FIN KENNEDY

Fin is a graduate of the MA Writing for Performance programme at Goldsmiths College, London. His first play, *Protection*, was produced at Soho Theatre in 2003, where he was also Pearson writer-in-residence. His second play, *How to Disappear Completely and Never Be Found*, won the 38th Arts Council John Whiting Award, the first time in forty years that an unproduced play had won. It was subsequently commissioned by Samuel West for Sheffield Crucible and enjoyed a sell-out run, transferring to London in 2008. It has also been produced in Australia, New Zealand and the United States, and is becoming a firm favourite with amateur and student groups around the UK.

Fin's first play for teenagers, *Locked In*, a hip-hop musical about pirate radio, was produced by Half Moon Young People's Theatre in 2006 and 2008, and toured nationally. His second play for Half Moon, *We Are Shadows*, toured during autumn 2007. 2008 also saw Fin's first radio commission, *Caesar Price Our Lord*, for BBC Radio 4, which was transmitted in September of that year.

For the past five years he has been writer-in-residence at Mulberry School for Girls in Tower Hamlets, London, where he is co-founder of Mulberry Theatre Company, for whom he wrote *Mehndi Night* (2007), *Stolen Secrets* (2008) and *The Unravelling* (2009) which all premiered at the Edinburgh Fringe Festival. *The Urban Girl's Guide to Camping* premiered at Southwark Playhouse in 2010.

As well as writing plays, Fin also has many years of experience teaching playwrighting at secondary, sixth-form, undergraduate and postgraduate levels. He has worked for schools, youth clubs, local authorities and theatre education teams in inner London and b

Goldsmiths C

Other Titles in the Series

Fin Kennedy

HOW TO DISAPPEAR COMPLETELY AND NEVER BE FOUND

NICK HERN BOOKS

London

www.nickhernbooks.co.uk

A Nick Hern Book

How to Disappear Completely and Never Be Found first published in Great Britain in 2007 as a paperback original by Nick Hern Books Limited, The Glasshouse, 49a Goldhawk Road, London W12 8QP

Reprinted 2008, 2010, 2011, 2012

How to Disappear Completely and Never Be Found copyright © 2007 Fin Kennedy

Fin Kennedy has asserted his moral right to be identified as the author of this work

Cover image by John Atkin, WPA Pinfold
Cover designed by Ned Hoste, 2H

Typeset by Country Setting, Kingsdown, Kent CT14 8ES
Printed and bound in Great Britain by CPI Antony Rowe, Chippenham, Wiltshire

A CIP catalogue record for this book is available from the British Library

ISBN 978 1 85459 964 3

Introduction

by Fin Kennedy

He looks like an ordinary guy. Short brown hair, brown eyes, small sideburns. An open and approachable face, smiling a big cheesy grin for the camera. It's the caption that makes you look twice: 'Age 26, was last seen in Retford, Notts on the 4th Feb 2000. After an evening with friends, Nick left in his blue Ford Escort. He is thought to have driven south.'

You carry on browsing. A mum of three, an Indian grandfather, a backpacker, a tattooed rocker, a city worker, a paediatrician. Gallery after gallery of smiling faces, ordinary people leading untroubled lives. Only something must have gone wrong. Because these snaps were the last time they were ever seen.

This is the unsettling experience of looking through the cases listed on the website of the National Missing Person's Helpline (NMPH), and it's where this play was born. I was instantly captivated. Who were these people? Why did they do it? And more to the point – how?

Some further research revealed some startling facts. It is estimated that between 100,000 and 250,000 people are reported missing to the police in the UK every single year. The Home Office puts the figure at 210,000. Many of these are children absconding from care, and many turn up within 72 hours, but many thousands do not. In 1999, 27,570 missing persons cases were reported to London's Metropolitan Police alone (the incidence appears to be higher in urban areas). A 2003 study* found that very few of these – less than 1% – are due to forced abduction or other crimes. Around one third are thought to have 'drifted' out of touch with friends and family, either through transient lifestyles, mental health problems or drug or alcohol addiction. A staggering two-thirds suffer from none of these, and when traced say they did it deliberately. This seemed to me to be an epidemic. I arranged to visit the NMPH to find out more.

* *Lost From View: Missing Persons in the UK*, Biehal, Mitchell and Wade, Policy Press 2003. All statistics quoted are from here

I meet Sophie Woodforde, a friendly press officer in her thirties, who talks me through what they do.' The Helpline was established as a charity in 1992 to advise and support missing people and those who are left behind. We hold the most detailed 'missing' database in the country. We do offer our services to organisations outside the family circle: the police, social workers, hospitals, care homes; but first and foremost we support families. The distress experienced during the initial weeks is when they need us most. State agencies such as the police are often unable to help, leaving NMPH to fill the gap.'

I ask her if there is a 'type' – a typical missing case they see time and time again. Straight away she replies, 'Yes, white male, late twenties or early thirties, good job in the private sector, suffers some kind of crisis, maybe personal, maybe financial, maybe both.' She snaps her fingers like a magician doing a trick: 'Disappears overnight.' I ask her why she thinks this is. 'I don't really know. Perhaps they've got the resources to pull it off.'

A few days later I meet a softly-spoken police officer, PC Rupert Plummer of the Met Police 'Mispers' team based in Clapham. His work starts at the other end, when a body turns up with no ID and they have to work out who they were. He shows me some pretty grim pictures before flooring me with another statistic: apparently an average of eighty bodies a year are retrieved from the Thames. That's nearly two a week. You rarely hear about them. Once again, a significant proportion of them are young men. When I ask him why, he sighs and looks a bit sad. 'They take more risks I suppose.'

Some books I had ordered began to arrive. Small underground publishers in America sell titles like: *The Modern Identity Changer*, *Advanced Fugitive*, or my favourite: *How to Disappear Completely and Never Be Found*. In the States at least, disappearing seems to have spawned a cottage industry in books, websites and private detectives. Sounding distinctly salesman-like, they know their market and promise much – dreams of freedom, a life in the sun, turning the system around on itself. Discovering who you 'really' are, outside of the bureaucratic machine. For a tiny but important moment, I feel tempted.

An idea begins to form in my mind. Facts and figures aside, this phenomenon speaks to me of something deeper than relationship break-ups and debt. It seems to go to the very heart of how we define ourselves. Leaving one's former identity behind and starting over seems to be an almost existential act; a yearning for good faith in a world which fetishises the fake. What makes you authentic? And how do you know you're real? These may not be new questions, but they are more relevant than ever, and no less terrifying – or unanswerable.

Those of a religious persuasion might say that we are all made in God's image and that it is He who forms us and decides our fate. The NMPH might say that it is family who defines us, and who continue to define us after we are gone. A pathologist might argue that we are nothing more than our bodies; a mass of tissue testifying to the lives we led and the deaths we encountered, through the scars we carry from each. Whilst the dodgy guide-books from America would have you believe your identity is simply a series of forms, certificates and computer files, open to manipulation in whatever way you see fit. Either way, the fact remains that all of us are only ever one step away from disappearing. Once you've made up your mind, the rest really isn't that hard.

I'd like to dedicate this play to those who have pulled it off. To the missing. The army of silent souls who walk among us.

I hope you find what you are looking for.

Acknowledgements

This play would not have come into being were it not for the generous assistance of the following people, to whom I owe a debt of gratitude:

Sarah Dickenson, John Ginman, Jaime Taylor, Sophie Woodforde and the National Missing Persons Helpline, PC Rupert Plummer and the Metropolitan Police Missing Person's Unit, Fr. Alexander Sherbrooke, The Connection Homeless Project at St Martin's, Rob Young, Joe Phillips, Michael Attenborough, Charles Hart and the Arts Council England's 38th John Whiting Playwriting Award panel, Mehmet Ergan and the NT Studio, Lloyd Trott and RADA, Jon Spooner, Ellie Jones, Samuel West and all at Sheffield Theatres.

How to Disappear Completely and Never Be Found was first performed at the Crucible Studio, Sheffield, on 23 March 2007, with the following cast:

CHARLIE/ADAM	William Ash
MIKE/TUBE MAN/ROBERT	Richard Bremmer
SOPHIE	Siân Rees
DOCTOR/ELLIE/NURSE	Esther Ruth Elliott
ERIC/DANNY/PRIEST	Steve Hansell

Other parts played by member of the company

Director   Ellie Jones
Designer   Ellen Cairns
Lighting Designer   Chris Davey
Sound Designer   Nicholas Briggs
Movement Director   Vik Sivalingam

HOW TO DISAPPEAR COMPLETELY
AND NEVER BE FOUND

Fin Kennedy

Characters

OLDER MAN, *fifties*
YOUNG WOMAN, *twenties*
WOMAN, *thirties*
MAN, *thirties*
CHARLIE, *thirties*
TUBE MAN, *fifties*
DOCTOR, *thirties*
ROBERT, *fifties*
ELLIE, *thirties*
AMERICAN CLIENT 1, *fifties*
AMERICAN CLIENT 2, *thirties*
ERIC, *thirties*
PARTY PEOPLE 1, 2 & 3
SOPHIE, *thirties*
DANNY, *thirties*
MIKE, *fifties*
ANGELINA, *thirties*
ADAM, *thirties*
PRIEST, *thirties*
BUREAUCRATS 1, 2 & 3
LANDLORD, *forties*
NURSE, *thirties*
PAWN MAN, *fifties*
MEDICAL STUDENTS
DEAD BODIES
YEVTSYE, *thirties*
MAN/BARRY, *thirties*

VOICES, *various male and female on voicemail*

The play has been arranged for five actors. The following are to double:

CHARLIE / ADAM

OLDER MAN / TUBE MAN / ROBERT / AMERICAN CLIENT 1 / PARTY PERSON 3 / MIKE / OLDER MEN'S VOICES 1 AND 2 / PAWN MAN

WOMAN / DOCTOR / ELLIE / ANGELINA / PARTY PERSON 1 / BUREAUCRAT 1 / BUREAUCRAT 3 / NURSE / WOMAN'S VOICE / OLDER WOMAN'S VOICE / YEVTSYE

MAN / ERIC / DANNY / AMERICAN CLIENT 2 / PRIEST / PARTY PERSON 2 / BUREAUCRAT 2 / MAN'S VOICE 1 / LANDLORD / MAN'S VOICE 2

Note: SOPHIE *does not double*

This text went to press before the end of rehearsals so may differ slightly from the play as performed.

ACT ONE

Darkness.

The sound of radio static, fading up and down as if scrolling through a frequency.

OLDER MAN. An amateur magician steps out onto the porch for a late-night cigarette. He discovers he has run out, so goes to the shop at the end of the street. His family expect him to be gone for ten minutes.

YOUNG WOMAN. A commercial fisherman goes out one day on the open sea, alone. The following day, his boat is found upside down on a remote beach. For a while, his wife and young daughter receive silent phone calls.

WOMAN. An actress and model fails to find a cab following a corporate party on New Year's Eve. She removes her high heels and decides to walk. CCTV catches her stumbling north. Her ansaphone greeting is erased.

MAN. An Anglican priest excuses himself during the Sunday service on the grounds of ill health. He walks down the aisle, through the graveyard, and out onto the dual carriageway.

OLDER MAN. A homeless man falls from a pier in a fog of drink and drugs. Found in just underpants and an overcoat, his body lies unclaimed for six months before being cremated in a state ceremony. A pathologist and a cleaner attend.

YOUNG WOMAN. An issue clerk working for the Passport Office misses her connecting flight in Bangkok. Regular e-mail updates to friends and family cease.

WOMAN. A fortune-teller from Eastern Europe washes up on an unfamiliar beach at night. She is last seen heading along the cliffs, towards the lights of a small coastal town, blinking in the rain.

MAN. Security footage captures a successful advertising executive running from the office one morning and out into the city traffic. He leaves his jacket on the back of his chair, and a cremation urn on his desk. Colleagues report him not having slept for over a week.

The static fades into the sound of rain falling against a window.

A digital bedside alarm goes off.

In the darkness, CHARLIE *hits a button.*

The alarm stops and a staccato electronic voice speaks.

ELECTRONIC VOICE. Five – forty – eight – a.m. Wednesday.

CHARLIE. You open your eyes, and it's dark. In the darkness, your head aches. In the darkness, your mouth is dry. You get up, and light a fag.

Outside, it's dark. Oily rain pisses down the window in fat black veins. You put your slippers on. They're cold. You scuff into the kitchen, feel for the kettle and the tap. A car alarm goes off in the street.

The sound of a distant car alarm. The rain steps up a notch.

In the darkness, you have a piss. In the darkness, you brush your teeth. In the darkness, you look in the mirror.

You look in the mirror.

You look in the mirror.

And things. Are about. To explode.

The sudden sound of a Tube train at high speed.

CHARLIE *faints. The others catch him. They guide him to a chair. Someone places a cremation urn on the ground next to him.*

TUBE MAN *stays with him. The radio static fades into that of a detuned portable radio that is hissing nearby.*

A table is strewn with mobile phones, wallets, umbrellas and other personal items. A straggly bit of tinsel hangs somewhere in an attempt at seasonal decoration.

TUBE MAN *hands* CHARLIE *a glass of water.*

TUBE MAN. Feeling better?

CHARLIE. I dunno.

TUBE MAN. Well, that's no good.

CHARLIE. I dunno what happened.

TUBE MAN. You fainted.

CHARLIE. Yeah.

TUBE MAN. It happens.

CHARLIE. Not normally.

TUBE MAN. It does with women. Old ones mostly. Here.

He hands CHARLIE *a damp cloth.*

CHARLIE. What?

TUBE MAN. For your head.

CHARLIE. Oh.

CHARLIE *feels his head. He looks at his fingers. There is red blood.*

TUBE MAN. Must've tapped it as you fell.

CHARLIE. Must've.

He takes the cloth.

TUBE MAN. Happens in summer mostly.

CHARLIE. What?

TUBE MAN. Summer's when we mostly get it.

CHARLIE. Get what?

TUBE MAN. Fainting.

CHARLIE. Oh.

TUBE MAN. We get it a lot then.

CHARLIE. Right.

TUBE MAN. But not in winter.

CHARLIE. No.

TUBE MAN. In summer it's the heat. We like to think it doesn't get hot in this country. But it does. But it's freezing today. You must be ill. Maybe you have a tumour. A tumour in your brain.

CHARLIE. I'm gonna be late for work.

CHARLIE stands unsteadily and looks as if he might drop again.

TUBE MAN. Uh uh uh. It's okay. Take your time.

TUBE MAN helps CHARLIE sit back down, then goes to fiddle with the radio. He can't get a signal.

CHARLIE. Fuck. I dunno what's wrong with me.

TUBE MAN. It's the sales.

CHARLIE. What?

TUBE MAN. January sales. All them bargain-hunters.

CHARLIE. I feel sick.

TUBE MAN. It's a funny time, between Christmas and New Year. No man's land. People just milling about.

CHARLIE. I haven't been sleeping.

TUBE MAN. Ah, well then.

CHARLIE. I'm a bit. Everything's a bit.

CHARLIE holds out the cloth.

Does my blood look a funny colour to you?

TUBE MAN. Around now is the peak time for Tube suicides. Eight a.m. No one knows why. This fact interests me.

CHARLIE. Does it.

TUBE MAN. Yes. I think sometimes, on the way to work, people just decide they can't face any more.

You were lucky. It could've been a lot worse.

You take as long as you need.

CHARLIE takes in his surroundings.

CHARLIE. Where are we?

TUBE MAN. Lost Property.

CHARLIE. I mean which station?

TUBE MAN. Oh. Embankment.

CHARLIE. What am I doing here? I never come this way.

TUBE MAN gives up on the radio.

TUBE MAN. Sod it.

CHARLIE. Aren't we underground?

TUBE MAN. Only six feet.

CHARLIE. Well, you won't get a signal then, will you?

TUBE MAN. Phones still work.

He gestures at the phones on the table in front of him.

Bloody things.

He leaves the radio hissing and goes to his desk.

Don't mind me. I've one or two things to be getting on with.

CHARLIE. You gonna leave that noise going?

TUBE MAN. It's all the company I've got.

CHARLIE. I'm here.

TUBE MAN. No. You're just passing through.

TUBE MAN begins sorting through the items on the table. He puts them into large drawers in the wall behind him – mobiles in one, wallets in another, umbrellas in another, etc.

A Tube train rumbles in the background. It gets louder during the following:

You have a nice Christmas, then?

CHARLIE. I cremated my mother.

TUBE MAN. Oh. (*Pause*.) Was she dead?

CHARLIE. Yeah.

TUBE MAN. Just as well.

CHARLIE. It was an open casket. They'd put make-up on her. But she still looked dead.

TUBE MAN. I had a nice quiet one with the missus.

TUBE MAN *indicates the urn*.

That her there?

CHARLIE *notices the urn next to him, as if for the first time*.

CHARLIE. Yeah.

TUBE MAN. You off to scatter her?

CHARLIE. No I'm – I'm going to work.

TUBE MAN *gives him a funny look and goes back to his filing*.

You collect a lot of shit here.

TUBE MAN. I don't collect it, people leave it.

CHARLIE. Yeah, I know.

TUBE MAN. Other people hand it in.

CHARLIE. Yeah, I know that.

TUBE MAN. When I first started it was mostly umbrellas. Thousands of umbrellas. Enough to survive a flood. Now it's mostly portable phones.

CHARLIE. Could I get –

TUBE MAN. *Hundreds* of portable phones.

CHARLIE. Yeah.

TUBE MAN. Never claimed.

CHARLIE. No, I can imagine.

TUBE MAN. Sometimes they all ring at once.

CHARLIE. Really?

TUBE MAN. We're just a holding room, of course. The main
  office in Baker Street gets a thousand items a day.

CHARLIE. That's a lot.

TUBE MAN. People should be more careful.

CHARLIE. Could I get another glass of water?

  *The train noise is so loud he has to shout this last line. The
  lights flicker.*

  He gestures with his empty glass.

  TUBE MAN *nods, takes it from him and goes off to fill it.
  The Tube noise subsides.*

  While TUBE MAN *is offstage,* CHARLIE *sifts through
  some of the lost items on the desk.*

TUBE MAN (*off*). Do you know what I always say?

CHARLIE. What's that?

TUBE MAN (*off*). You can tell the soul of a nation from the
  stuff that it loses.

CHARLIE. Huh. I like that.

  CHARLIE *toys with a gold watch he has found.*

TUBE MAN (*off*). Yes, good, isn't it? I thought about getting
  them to put it on a poster.

CHARLIE. That'd look good on a poster. I work in marketing,
  and I can tell you that'd look good.

TUBE MAN (*off*). I meant more as a public information
  campaign. To make people more careful.

  CHARLIE *pockets the gold watch just as* TUBE MAN
  comes back through with the water.

  TUBE MAN *hands him the glass.* CHARLIE *isn't sure if
  he's been seen.*

CHARLIE. Cheers.

TUBE MAN. You don't mind me prattling on, do you?

CHARLIE. Um, no.

TUBE MAN. I don't get many visitors. And I can see you like detritus.

CHARLIE. I wasn't –

TUBE MAN. No, I know. You're not the sort. But now you have to listen to me, and pretend to be interested in case I report you for theft.

Pause.

Yes, I used to think a lot about the decline of the umbrella. I'd look at all the umbrellas I used to get, armfuls and armfuls of them, and I'd ask myself 'What does this say about our Great Nation?' What do you think it says?

CHARLIE. Er. That it rains a lot.

TUBE MAN. It says caution, it says preparation, it says pragmatism. Quiet, ordered lives in which nothing could be more distressing than to get rained on. The umbrella, the safety net of the nation. And now the shrill, self-promoting portable phone has taken its place.

You're not looking very interested.

CHARLIE. Oh I am. Very. I'm very interested. I think you're onto something.

TUBE MAN. Do you. Do you.

CHARLIE. Uh-huh.

TUBE MAN. Nothing but thousands upon thousands of umbrellas throughout the twentieth century. Then a brief period when we lost an Empire.

CHARLIE. Probably left it on the Central Line.

TUBE MAN. People are particularly careless on the Central Line.

CHARLIE. Are they.

TUBE MAN. And now the portable phone.

CHARLIE. Fuck, I've just remembered. It was a bag.

TUBE MAN. What?

CHARLIE. There was an abandoned bag, that's why I went funny.

TUBE MAN. What do you mean?

CHARLIE. He was there next to me, bloke with a carrier bag at his feet. He got out at Temple and left it there. And the fear, the bolt of fear must just have – And what with the crowds and. Fuck. You have to tell someone. He was dark.

TUBE MAN. Dark.

CHARLIE. Dark-skinned.

TUBE MAN. Foreign.

CHARLIE. I dunno, probably.

TUBE MAN. A dark-skinned man leaves his lunch on the District Line. A chicken sandwich, a mouldy banana and a Twix. And the world goes into spasm.

CHARLIE. I'm just. We're on a heightened alert.

TUBE MAN. They blow us up because they say we're the infidel. That we're evil. Crazed. Look around you. Look around you in this town and tell me. Do you see *any sign* of God? Well, do you?

CHARLIE. I. Can't say I've looked.

TUBE MAN. Well, start. Because maybe they're right. Maybe we *are* the infidel. Maybe we're all festering in Hell.

CHARLIE. I. Really have to get going.

TUBE MAN. Let 'em get on with it, that's what I say. Stinking rotten heap. Blow it up. Blow it all up.

CHARLIE. I take it this isn't the official position of London Transport.

One of the mobile phones in the pile on the table begins to ring.

TUBE MAN. Excuse me one moment.

*TUBE MAN finds the ringing phone and answers it.
CHARLIE gathers his things, but stops as he hears the
following.*

Hello.

No, no, it isn't.

I'm afraid he's no longer with us.

No, it was tragic. I'm surprised you haven't heard.

On the District Line. Terrible mess.

CHARLIE. Hey.

TUBE MAN. I'm Peter, I guard the gates up here. You-know-
who won't allow phones inside.

He hangs up and tosses the phone down.

CHARLIE. I've heard of Scrooge, but fuckin 'ell. You take it
to a whole new level.

TUBE MAN. Just my little joke.

CHARLIE. You need to get out more.

TUBE MAN. People should be more careful.

CHARLIE. Losin your phone isn't fun.

TUBE MAN. Oh, it's traumatising. I see it. I hear it. The social
damage wrought by such a massive loss. Losing a brolly
meant getting wet but now – *now*. The never-heard voicemail
messages cancelling the evening's entertainment, the texts
requesting the purchase of coffee and dishwasher powder on
the way home, the DVD rental suggestions, the takeaway
pizza orders, the location requests, the progress reports, the
rising tone of panic, the pleas to just let me know you're
okay, the puzzlement, the frustration, the rage: 'I don't
understand, I don't understand why you're not answering,'
the *begging* to answer, just for the love of God please just
answer the fucking *phone* – for you are nothing – *nothing* –
so long as you are *quiet*.

Believe me. I see it all.

CHARLIE *picks up the urn*.

CHARLIE. I have to go.

TUBE MAN. Think of all the record-breaking high scores at Snake that have to be abandoned, never to be regained. Is this what we're defending so jealously?

CHARLIE. Thanks for the water.

TUBE MAN. Haven't you forgotten something?

CHARLIE. What?

TUBE MAN *produces the gold watch*. CHARLIE *checks his pockets. It isn't there*.

TUBE MAN. We're all thieves.

CHARLIE. How did you do that?

TUBE MAN. Just my little trick. Allow an old man that.

TUBE MAN *throws it to* CHARLIE, *who catches it*.

Keep it. Happy New Year. I'm sorry about your mum.

CHARLIE. Thanks.

TUBE MAN. Was it sudden?

CHARLIE. Yeah. Yeah, it was.

TUBE MAN. Go and get some sleep.

They part. CHARLIE *puts the watch on his wrist*.

The phones on the table all ring at once.

After a moment, a voicemail message in.

CHARLIE. Hi, it's me. Sorry I can't get to the phone, probably in a meeting. You know what to do.

A long beep.

ELLIE. Charlie, it's Ellie. Not sure where you are. Just a reminder I'll be sitting in with you and the Americans at half past. And try and keep your phone on, alright? It's a big building.

*The sound of radio static fades up. Snatches of excitable
chatter can almost be made out amongst it.*

CHARLIE. You could go in straight away. Grovel out an
apology. Check the two hundred e-mails in your inbox. Try
to come up with better ways of selling ice cream to men in
their forties. But you don't. You put off work another
quarter of an hour with a visit to the company doctor.

Quarter of an hour. Bliss.

The DOCTOR *comes in.* CHARLIE *puts down the urn.*

DOCTOR. You were lucky, someone cancelled. You should
book.

CHARLIE. Don't be like that, I'm paying.

DOCTOR. The company's paying.

CHARLIE. It's an emergency.

DOCTOR. I'll be the judge of that. Now be quiet.

She listens to CHARLIE's *chest.*

Heart disease?

CHARLIE. Shit, is it?

DOCTOR. Do you have any history of heart disease?

CHARLIE. Oh. No.

DOCTOR. Murmurs or palpitations?

CHARLIE. No.

DOCTOR. Epilepsy?

CHARLIE. No.

DOCTOR. Diabetes?

CHARLIE. No.

DOCTOR. Low blood pressure?

CHARLIE. Don't think so.

DOCTOR. Yes or no?

CHARLIE. No.

DOCTOR *examines* CHARLIE*'s eyes*.

DOCTOR. Any recent head injuries?

CHARLIE. A tap as I fell. Nothing before.

She examines his head injury briefly.

Does it. Does it look like the right colour?

DOCTOR. What?

CHARLIE. My blood. Does it look. My blood's been gettin paler.

DOCTOR. Don't be ridiculous.

CHARLIE. I'm not.

DOCTOR (*of the wound*). It's nothing.

CHARLIE. No?

DOCTOR. No.

CHARLIE. Oh.

DOCTOR. Anything that might have caused internal bleeding?

CHARLIE. No.

DOCTOR. Did you experience any dizziness or nausea before you passed out?

CHARLIE. I don't think so, I just went.

DOCTOR. Upset stomach?

CHARLIE. Yes, I felt sick.

DOCTOR. Shortness of breath?

CHARLIE. Don't think so.

DOCTOR. Pressure in the chest?

CHARLIE. No.

DOCTOR. Is there any chance that you could be pregnant?

CHARLIE. Excuse me?

DOCTOR. Are you on medication?

CHARLIE. No.

DOCTOR. Illegal substances?

CHARLIE. Only coke.

DOCTOR. Are you addicted?

CHARLIE. No more than anyone else in the building.

DOCTOR. Lay off it unless we prescribe it. Alcohol?

CHARLIE. Yeah, cheers, I wouldn't mind a drink.

DOCTOR. You're an alcoholic?

CHARLIE. No, I just fancy a drink.

DOCTOR. And why might that be?

CHARLIE. I feel like shit.

DOCTOR. Can you be more specific?

CHARLIE. No.

DOCTOR. Any pain?

CHARLIE. Yes.

DOCTOR. Where?

CHARLIE. Everywhere.

DOCTOR. Do you eat breakfast?

CHARLIE. If I have time.

DOCTOR. Which is?

CHARLIE. Not often.

DOCTOR. You need a big breakfast. Cooked. Fried, preferably.
    Power you up for the day.

CHARLIE. Right.

DOCTOR. You have a weak heartbeat.

CHARLIE. Really?

DOCTOR. Yes.

CHARLIE. What does that mean?

DOCTOR. You need to drink more coffee.

CHARLIE. Right. How much?

DOCTOR. As much as you can. The company's approaching a very busy period, we'll be needing one hundred and ten per cent.

CHARLIE. Right.

DOCTOR looks at a chart with a zigzag line on it.

DOCTOR. How many hours have you worked this month?

CHARLIE. All of them.

DOCTOR. Your chart says you've only averaged eighty per cent.

CHARLIE. Christmas got in the way. I had to cremate my mother.

DOCTOR. That's no excuse. We need you here.

CHARLIE. I'm sorry.

DOCTOR. No problem. Here.

She hands him a jar of pills.

CHARLIE. What are these?

DOCTOR. To keep you awake.

CHARLIE. Right.

DOCTOR. And these.

Another jar.

To help you sleep.

CHARLIE. Thanks.

DOCTOR. Don't mix them up.

CHARLIE. I won't.

DOCTOR. Tell the next one to come in, would you?

CHARLIE. Right. Um. Do you have anything –

DOCTOR. What?

CHARLIE. I'm just not –

DOCTOR. What?

CHARLIE. It's just that. I'm not feeling very happy.

DOCTOR. You're depressed.

CHARLIE. I don't think so.

DOCTOR. It's very common.

CHARLIE. No.

DOCTOR. Nothing to be ashamed of.

CHARLIE. It's not that.

DOCTOR. Take these.

More pills.

CHARLIE. Listen. I don't think it's me.

DOCTOR. What?

CHARLIE. I don't think the problem lies with me. I think things might genuinely be shit.

DOCTOR. Look out the window. A staff Zen garden, fully landscaped. A water feature, an alfresco courtyard. A gym, a restaurant, a café, a crèche. There are even beds if you book in advance. You have everything. Everything you could possibly want.

CHARLIE. Look. Do you ever. Do you ever feel like what you see is just this thin surface? That if you push your finger in, that – that *membrane* would give way with a pop – like – like *cling film*. And then inside there's just this. Grey sludge.

DOCTOR. Pull yourself together. Take the pills. And get back to work.

CHARLIE *looks at the pills.* DOCTOR *goes.*

CHARLIE. You pull yourself together. You take the pills. You get back to work.

He has some of the pills.

ROBERT *enters and stands at a lectern.* CHARLIE *picks up the urn and waits nearby.*

ROBERT. Now. As you'll know, Red Consultancy is itself a major brand presence across a range of global service markets.

Life here is fast. Very fast. But fun. Some of you might feel the pressure, and that's good, that's healthy, we want you to enjoy that. We want you to succeed. We want you all to be winners.

It's for this reason that we have the monthly full-company meetings. It's at these that you'll be expected to detail your professional *and personal* targets for that month. If you're in debt, we want to know about it. If you're trying for a baby, we want to know about it. If your health's on the blink, we want to know about it. Because you have a new family now who may just be able to help. Welcome to the firm.

Okay, enough from me. You shouldn't be seeing me again unless you screw up. I'll hand you over now to one of our most hard-working Brand Managers. Charlie Hunt.

CHARLIE *steps up to the lectern holding the urn. A smattering of applause. He squints at the assembled crowd.*

There is a buzzing sound in the air, like feedback from the mic.

CHARLIE. You can't concentrate. Coordination's going. Trying to remember something that's been said but there's nothing. The world is sliding away, the air full of shiny stinging particles. You have this feeling of having left part of yourself behind. But you can't remember what.

AMERICAN CLIENT 1, AMERICAN CLIENT 2 *and* ELLIE *enter behind him.*

There is a scratching noise now, as well as the buzzing.

Your skin crawls. Your skin itches. Not just your skin but your muscles. It's like your muscles itch. You wanna rip them open and scratch at the sinews. You tense everything up and relax again. Tense, relax. Tense, relax. Clenching your teeth, your arms, stomach, legs, kneecaps, curling your feet. Feeling like your whole body might pop at any moment and that would be it.

AMERICAN CLIENT 1. Mr Hunt?

CHARLIE. And that fucking *noise*.

ELLIE. Charlie.

CHARLIE. Like feedback in your head.

ELLIE. Charlie.

CHARLIE. I just want some fucking sleep!

ELLIE. Charlie!

The noises subside, but don't go away entirely.

CHARLIE. Huh? Oh. Yeah. Sorry.

AMERICAN CLIENT 2. You were saying?

ELLIE (*of the urn*). What's that?

CHARLIE. Nothing.

CHARLIE *puts it down.*

AMERICAN CLIENT 1. You were saying?

CHARLIE. Yeah. Right. So. What is it that you sell again?

ELLIE. Oh, for goodness' sake.

AMERICAN CLIENT 1. Speed-dating.

CHARLIE. Of course.

AMERICAN CLIENT 2. Thirty dates in one night. You like?

CHARLIE. Sure. I like. So. Right. Yeah.

He uses a handheld button to scroll through some pictures on a screen – a PowerPoint presentation.

What we'd do first of all, and I'm talking viral marketing now, uh, text ads, yeah mobile – mobile *videos*, YouTube, word-of-mouth under-the-radar stuff, right, so there's no fucking escape, is is is –

ELLIE. Charlie.

CHARLIE. – we'd establish, establish the *Other*, that is, that is, what the alternative is for these people, that is, *not* falling in love, and and present *that* as the current state of affairs if things don't *change*.

AMERICAN CLIENT 1. Uh-huh.

AMERICAN CLIENT 2. I can work with that.

CHARLIE. The the existing *narrative* if you will, if people don't, if people can't, if people won't – take *control*.

AMERICAN CLIENT 1. Control is good.

AMERICAN CLIENT 2. We like control.

CHARLIE. So so so we're talking hourly Friday-night texts saying, 'Are you still at work, you sad git?', we're talking misery, loneliness, overwork, dark blues and browns and maroons and and *debt* – hard scary *debt* to some dodgy fuckers on an estate –

ELLIE. Charlie, please.

CHARLIE. And and and –

ELLIE (*to* CLIENTS). I apologise.

AMERICAN CLIENT 1. Not at all.

CHARLIE. – time –

AMERICAN CLIENT 2. It's inner-city.

CHARLIE. – time just being –

AMERICAN CLIENT 1. It speaks to me.

CHARLIE. – just fucking being *the* most *precious* thing – more than *money,* so much more because because because time *is* the new money – is that fucking up-there gold-dust thing that we all we all – we all – can anyone else hear that buzzing?

AMERICAN CLIENT 1. Huh?

CHARLIE. A buzzing noise.

AMERICAN CLIENT 1. I don't think so. Can *you* hear a buzzing?

AMERICAN CLIENT 2. I don't think so, sir.

AMERICAN CLIENT 1. Maybe your *electrics* need attention.

ELLIE. No one can hear a buzzing, Charlie. Are you sure you're alright?

CHARLIE. I'm fine, it's fine. So so a campaign emphasising the the *negative* – and offering *you* – offering – what the fuck are you called?

AMERICAN CLIENT 1. Quick Love.

AMERICAN CLIENT 2. Quick Love dot com.

ELLIE. Charlie, are you sure you don't want to perhaps –

CHARLIE. Brilliant yeah so *Quick* Love – like that that *name* is like the the the passport, the credit card, yeah the *credit card*, but not of money – no, not even of time, though that's a good idea –

AMERICAN CLIENT 1. Credit card of time.

AMERICAN CLIENT 2. I like.

CHARLIE. But but but Quick Love's *not* that, no –

AMERICAN CLIENTS 1/2. Oh.

CHARLIE. Quick Love is the the the credit card of *love*, of opportunity, of of of *Fate*. You get me?

AMERICAN CLIENT 1. I getcha.

AMERICAN CLIENT 2. Yuh.

CHARLIE. Yeah?

AMERICAN CLIENT 1. I think.

AMERICAN CLIENT 2. Yuh.

CHARLIE. Yeah?

AMERICAN CLIENT 1. Do you get him?

AMERICAN CLIENT 2. I don't think so, sir.

AMERICAN CLIENT 1. No?

AMERICAN CLIENT 2. No.

CHARLIE. No?

AMERICAN CLIENT 1. No, I don't get him.

AMERICAN CLIENT 2. I don't get him either.

AMERICAN CLIENT 1. I don't get him at all.

AMERICAN CLIENT 2. Mr Hunt, we don't get you at all.

CHARLIE. Fuck.

ELLIE. Charlie, I think you'd better take five.

CHARLIE. It's fine, no, I'm doing doing a *consultation*, Ellie,
outlining – what's what's – what we can, what we at Red
can – I'm almost there.

ELLIE. Charlie, just calm down.

CHARLIE. No, I'm calm I'm there I'm fine – we have to
remember – Ellie, Joe, you, whatever your name is, all of
you, what we have to remember is Attention, Interest,
Desire, Action, okay?

CHARLIE*'s nose has started to bleed.*

AMERICAN CLIENT 1. Okay.

AMERICAN CLIENT 2. Yuh.

AMERICAN CLIENT 1. I like that.

AMERICAN CLIENT 2. That makes more sense.

CHARLIE. The old formula yeah, but it's sound so so so let's
say let's say then – *then* we'd have the mobile video ad sent
out at *rush* hour and we'd open with with with – fuck!

He rubs at his nose. Blood seeps out.

ELLIE. Oh my God.

CHARLIE. So then we'd open we'd have we'd cut to a picture yeah – zooming in on on a picture of of of –

ELLIE. Charlie, you're bleeding.

CHARLIE. – some dolly bird in the rain in the inner city yeah, heavy lashing rain like like an oil slick, and it's early and bitter and she's on her way in to work and the rain pounds into her face like sludge and and and her mouth's all open and the water's all it's all sort of running down her chin and and –

Blood runs down CHARLIE's *chin.*

ELLIE. Charlie!

AMERICAN CLIENT 1. Jesus lady!

AMERICAN CLIENT 2. Wouldya let the man speak – he's trying to make a pitch!

AMERICAN CLIENT 1. And I'm liking what I'm hearing.

AMERICAN CLIENT 2. So am I.

AMERICAN CLIENT 1. Any man can make a pitch like that with blood pouring out of his face.

AMERICAN CLIENT 2. In the middle of a breakdown.

AMERICAN CLIENT 1. Or whatever the fuck he's having.

AMERICAN CLIENT 2. Yuh.

AMERICAN CLIENT 1. Gets my attention.

AMERICAN CLIENT 2. He gets our attention.

AMERICAN CLIENT 1. Here.

AMERICAN CLIENT 2. Here.

They each hand CHARLIE *a handkerchief.*

CHARLIE. Thanks.

AMERICAN CLIENT 1. You're welcome.

AMERICAN CLIENT 2. Don't mention it.

AMERICAN CLIENT 1. Not at all.

AMERICAN CLIENT 2. My pleasure.

AMERICAN CLIENT 1. Now pitch goddammit.

AMERICAN CLIENT 2. Pitch.

AMERICAN CLIENT 1. Pitch.

AMERICAN CLIENT 2. Pitch!

The buzzing static cranks up.

Mobile phones ring.

CHARLIE *cries out and clutches at his head.*

AMERICAN CLIENT 1. He seemed confused.

AMERICAN CLIENT 2. He was an asshole.

AMERICAN CLIENT 1. I didn't like his *manner*.

AMERICAN CLIENT 2. It was manic.

AMERICAN CLIENT 1. You're right.

AMERICAN CLIENT 2. A manic manner.

AMERICAN CLIENT 1. He had these eyes.

AMERICAN CLIENT 2. Wild.

AMERICAN CLIENT 1. Like a bum.

AMERICAN CLIENT 2. Like a bum on the street who asks your for change.

AMERICAN CLIENT 1. Everyone works hard, but Jesus.

AMERICAN CLIENT 2. Jesus. You *deal* with it.

AMERICAN CLIENT 1. I didn't like his suit. It was cheap.

AMERICAN CLIENT 2. I didn't like his eyes.

AMERICAN CLIENT 1. I didn't like his face.

AMERICAN CLIENT 2. He was an asshole.

AMERICAN CLIENT 1. The guy was a goddam asshole.

CHARLIE *grabs the urn and leaves.*

CHARLIE. Five more hours of this and your body's crying out for sleep. But your head needs to get pissed. *So* badly. You pop another wake-up pill and meet Eric for lunch.

CHARLIE *has another pill.* ERIC *brings two pints over.*

ERIC. The average working lunch break in the UK is seventeen minutes. On average. But not advertising. Do you know how long we get?

CHARLIE. No.

ERIC. Four-and-a-half minutes. That's why we're on the big bucks. So hurry the fuck up.

ERIC *downs most of his pint. Then he notices the pills* CHARLIE *is holding.*

What are they?

CHARLIE. Oh. Nothing.

ERIC. They legal?

CHARLIE. Yeah.

ERIC. Ah, I'm not interested. Now. Chunter.

CHARLIE. Eh?

ERIC. Yes.

CHARLIE. What?

ERIC. Your behaviour's been noticed.

CHARLIE. How – how do you mean?

ERIC (*indicating the urn*). Well, what the fuck is this?

CHARLIE. It's. It's my mum.

ERIC. I can see that. Why have you brought her into work?

CHARLIE. I didn't. I just. She just.

ERIC. What? Followed you?

CHARLIE. I. I.

ERIC. You've been carrying her round. Alison says it makes her feel sick.

CHARLIE. I'm sorry.

ERIC. Have you fucking lost it or what?

CHARLIE. I don't know.

ERIC. What would your poor mother say if she could see you now?

CHARLIE. I don't know.

ERIC. What *do* you know?

CHARLIE. I.

ERIC (*checks watch*). Two minutes.

CHARLIE. I haven't been sleeping.

ERIC. So? Look, give that here.

> ERIC *tries to take the urn.* CHARLIE *resists.*

CHARLIE. Get off.

ERIC. We could scatter her right now, get it out the way.

CHARLIE (*shouts*). Get off!

> ERIC *backs off. Pause.*

ERIC. Everyone's looking over now, you prick.

CHARLIE. Eric.

ERIC. What?

CHARLIE. Do you ever. Do you ever feel like everything's fake?

ERIC. Eh?

CHARLIE. Like this place. It looks like an old pub but it wasn't here last year.

ERIC. That's branding, mate. That's why we're on the big bucks. You just gotta believe.

CHARLIE. I do believe.

ERIC. Do you? I'm not sure you do.

CHARLIE. I do.

ERIC. Questions are being asked, Charlie.

CHARLIE. It's fine.

ERIC. I mean, do you wanna throw all this away?

CHARLIE. No.

ERIC. Course you don't. Who would? We're the bollocks. We are living the dream. Everyone wants to be us. Even us.

ERIC *laughs*.

If you can't hack the pace you know what you gotta do, don't ya?

CHARLIE. Yeah. Yeah thanks, Eric.

ERIC *checks his watch. Radio static hisses*.

ERIC. Time's up.

CHARLIE. Right.

ERIC. See you tonight, yeah?

CHARLIE. Yeah.

ERIC. New year, new life. (*Of the urn*.) Don't bring that.

ERIC *downs his drink and goes*.

CHARLIE *pretends to down his while* ERIC *is there, then stops when* ERIC *has gone*.

CHARLIE *looks ill. He finds a surface for the urn and puts it down*.

CHARLIE. You go back to work. Throw up. Put in another ten hours. Try and avoid any mirrors.

He smoothes his hair down.

He pops another pill.

Then you pop another wake-up pill and go to a party.

The static fades into noise of a rowdy party crowd.

PARTY PEOPLE 1, 2 *and* 3 *appear. They hold drinks and laugh loudly.*

SOPHIE *is in the background, silently watching.*

There's some place in Islington with a rooftop terrace that they've hired for a corporate launch. Someone's put ten grand behind the bar so everyone's steamin. Models mix with copywriters mix with corporate finance.

You look at the lights of the buildings, tearing open the darkness like a filthy neon smile. People are talkin. It's cold.

CHARLIE *grabs a glass from a passing* WAITER *and downs it. He grabs another.*

PARTY PERSON 1. What do *you* do?

PARTY PERSON 2. What do *you* do?

PARTY PERSON 3. What do *you* do?

PARTY PERSON 1. I'm an actress. I was a child star in cereal adverts but it was too much too young. I turned to drink and smack at fourteen.

PARTY PERSON 2. A tragedy.

PARTY PERSON 1. But I pulled myself back from the brink. Did corporate videos and cardigan catalogues. And now tonight.

PARTY PERSON 3. A triumph of the human spirit.

PARTY PERSON 1. I like to think so.

PARTY PERSON 2. I *love* the campaign. It's going to be massive.

PARTY PERSON 1. You're a sweetie.

PARTY PERSON 3. Which cereal?

PARTY PERSON 1 (*to* PARTY PERSON 2). What do *you* do?

PARTY PERSON 2. I work for the bank underwriting all this.

PARTY PERSON 1. A money man.

PARTY PERSON 2. Well. I normally specialise in asset-stripping small African countries and dollarising their economies.

PARTY PERSON 3. Interesting.

PARTY PERSON 2. Not really. I'm just here for the bubbly. (*To* PARTY PERSON 3.) What do *you* do?

PARTY PERSON 3. I wrote her script.

PARTY PERSON 1. How do you mean?

PARTY PERSON 3. Copywriter.

PARTY PERSON 1. Oh, from the agency! Darling, you should've said.

PARTY PERSON 3. Well. I'm just here for the bubbly too.

PARTY PERSON 2. So all that signet-into-swan stuff –

PARTY PERSON 3. Was mine, yes.

PARTY PERSON 1. I love that image.

PARTY PERSON 2. Let's hope it sells.

PARTY PERSON 1. Oh, don't be mean.

PARTY PERSON 2. It's a big investment.

PARTY PERSON 1. The caterpillar into the butterfly, the promise of a fresh start. Does it for me.

PARTY PERSON 3 (*pouring more champagne*). It's tried and tested, I wouldn't worry yourself overly.

PARTY PERSON 2. Oh I won't, it's not my money.

PARTY PERSON 1. So tell me, am I the butterpillar or the catterfly?

PARTY PERSON 3. I'm sorry?

PARTY PERSON 1. I mean –

PARTY PERSON 2. Are you the what?

PARTY PERSON 1. Oh my God I'm so drunk.

They laugh.

CHARLIE. You try and get their attention, but they're talking about something else. Hi.

PARTY PERSON 1 (*furtively*). No one from the Laboratoire's around are they?

PARTY PERSON 3. Can't see them.

PARTY PERSON 2. Wouldn't recognise them.

PARTY PERSON 1. Cos between you and me, their fucking foundation makes my skin flare up.

CHARLIE. Hi, I'm Charlie.

PARTY PERSON 2. Oh God, really?

PARTY PERSON 3. Don't tell him that.

PARTY PERSON 1. I thought they shoved it in rabbits' eyes to make sure.

PARTY PERSON 2. They do.

PARTY PERSON 1. Well, they've got some tough rabbits.

CHARLIE. Hi, I'm Charlie. I haven't slept for over a week. But the conversation's moved on.

PARTY PERSON 2. I can't stand relaxing. I booked a two-week holiday last summer and came back after four days.

PARTY PERSON 1. You're going away with the wrong people, darling.

PARTY PERSON 3. Oh, I went back to Tuscany this year and it's gone to the fucking dogs, I can tell you.

PARTY PERSON 1. Oh, it's a travesty.

PARTY PERSON 3. A tragedy.

CHARLIE. Oi!

They stop and look at him.

My my my name's Charlie. I'm twenty-nine. I don't have any hobbies. I just work. I never get to meet anyone or go anywhere so I don't have any funny stories.

PARTY PERSON 1. He looked pissed.

PARTY PERSON 2. Bloodshot.

PARTY PERSON 3. Ill-looking.

PARTY PERSON 1. Like he'd slobber on you if you got too close.

PARTY PERSON 2. Socially stunted.

PARTY PERSON 3. Not a lot of friends.

PARTY PERSON 1. Desperate.

PARTY PERSON 3. Lonely.

PARTY PERSON 2. A bad investment.

PARTY PERSON 1. A bad haircut.

PARTY PERSON 3. Probably owns a lot of porn.

PARTY PERSON 2. Optimistically buys condoms

PARTY PERSON 1. Then wanks into them

PARTY PERSON 2. Whilst drunk.

PARTY PERSON 3. I felt sorry for him.

PARTY PERSON 1. Oh shut up.

PARTY PERSON 2. He'd drug your drink.

PARTY PERSON 1. And fuck you in a Travelodge.

They laugh.

Some bells chime midnight and fireworks pop overhead.

Oh it's time! It's time!

A chorus of 'Auld Lang Syne' starts in the background. The PARTY PEOPLE *leave to join in.*

SOPHIE *goes over to* CHARLIE.

SOPHIE. Wow.

CHARLIE. What?

SOPHIE. People.

CHARLIE. Oh. Yeah.

SOPHIE. Is this who you spent your time with?

CHARLIE. Not by choice.

SOPHIE. That one over there. His skin looks like a sack holding him in.

CHARLIE. Huh. That's funny.

SOPHIE. Drowned people look like that.

CHARLIE. Do they?

SOPHIE. Uh-huh.

CHARLIE. That's. Interesting.

SOPHIE. Look at that.

CHARLIE. What?

SOPHIE. Up there.

CHARLIE. Oh. Yeah.

SOPHIE. They've branded the clouds.

CHARLIE. I know. I'm sorry, I haven't slept for a week and I'm really pissed.

SOPHIE. I know. And the cocktail of pills in your stomach is quite dangerous.

CHARLIE. Looking up's not very pleasant. What?

A huge firework lights up overhead. People cheer.

SOPHIE. Wow. How do they get writing inside a firework?

CHARLIE. With lots of money.

SOPHIE. How much?

CHARLIE. You don't wanna know.

SOPHIE. Happy New Year, then.

CHARLIE. Yeah.

SOPHIE. And all that.

CHARLIE. And all that.

SOPHIE. I'm Sophie.

She offers her hand. They shake.

CHARLIE. Hello, Sophie.

SOPHIE. And you are?

CHARLIE. Charlie.

SOPHIE. Charlie. Right. Aren't you going to ask me what I do?

CHARLIE. No.

He tries to take his hand back but she holds on to it. She indicates the watch on his wrist.

SOPHIE. Tell me about this watch.

CHARLIE. What?

SOPHIE. Where did you get it?

CHARLIE. What does it matter?

SOPHIE. Tell me.

CHARLIE. Why?

SOPHIE. Take it off.

CHARLIE. No.

SOPHIE. Look at the back. There's an engraving.

CHARLIE. I. Hadn't noticed.

CHARLIE takes the watch off and looks at the back.

'Harry Lewis.'

SOPHIE. That's my dad.

CHARLIE. Really?

SOPHIE. Yup.

CHARLIE. It's a common name.

SOPHIE. What else does it say?

CHARLIE. 'On your twenty-first.' It's gone all blurry. 'Twelfth of the seventh – '

SOPHIE. 1975.

CHARLIE. Right.

SOPHIE. Right.

Pause.

He was a fisherman. One night he went out on his own. His boat was found further up the coast, intact. How did you get his watch?

CHARLIE. Who *are* you?

SOPHIE. I'm a pathologist. Your body was retrieved from the Thames last night. You had no identification. I've been working all day to discover who you are.

CHARLIE. Have you drugged my drink?

SOPHIE. I can tell you had a stressful lifestyle because you have the beginnings of a stomach ulcer.

CHARLIE. You're one of those goth girls, right?

SOPHIE. Your liver shows signs of alcohol damage.

CHARLIE. Into death and stuff.

SOPHIE. Your stomach contents show a final meal of scampi and chips, which suggests that you might have been in a seaside town. Would that be right?

CHARLIE. I have had. A very long day.

SOPHIE. Your blood shows high levels of alcohol, cocaine –

CHARLIE. And you're doin my head in.

SOPHIE. – sleeping pills and anti-depressants.

CHARLIE. You know, at first you looked quite normal.

SOPHIE. You must have been in quite a state.

CHARLIE. I even quite fancied you.

SOPHIE. How did you break your knuckles?

CHARLIE. But now you've fucked it up.

SOPHIE. And get the slashes on your arms?

CHARLIE. This isn't happening.

SOPHIE. Touch the edges of your mouth. You see that foam? It's a mixture of water, air and mucus whipped up by respiratory efforts. It indicates that you were alive at the time of submersion.

CHARLIE. I feel sick.

SOPHIE. How did you get my father's watch?

CHARLIE. I'm leaving now, and going home to be sick. Then, if you leave me alone, I promise to get some sleep.

SOPHIE. Here's my card.

CHARLIE. What?

SOPHIE. I like you. You're different.

CHARLIE. Different to what?

SOPHIE. All the other dead people.

CHARLIE. Oh good. That's nice.

SOPHIE. Call me.

CHARLIE. You have a very unusual approach to dating.

SOPHIE. Call me.

CHARLIE. Right.

SOPHIE *goes*.

Fuckin hell.

He takes out one of the pill jars and has a few.

He checks the time on the watch.

You go home. Throw up. Have a painkiller, a leading brand. You watch the twenty-four-hour auction channel on cable.

Going. Going. Gone.

*He collapses onto a bed. Almost immediately, a bedside
alarm goes off. He hits it off.*

ELECTRONIC VOICE. Five – forty – eight – a.m. Thursday.

CHARLIE. You open your eyes, and it's dark. In the darkness,
your head aches. In the darkness, your mouth is dry. You get
up, and light a fag.

With a hangover so thick it's like bells ringing, you try and
piece together the evening. Work, obviously. Late finish,
as usual. Drinks, naturally. New recruits. Corporate launch.
More drinks, of course. Few lines of coke. People talking
too fast. Hazy from there on in. An empty wallet. A
smoker's cough. Bad dream about a girl and a watch.

You give up thinking and drink a can of lager on the way to
the station.

On the platform, the train is delayed. Some rain has fallen,
which no one could have foreseen in December. Your ex
texts. 'Great sex last night with fit new guy. Can I delete
your name from my phone cos his number won't fit in my
box? Happy New Year.' You consider ringing the bitch then
chucking your phone under a train. But you don't.

On the Tube the bright lights hurt your eyes. There's this
guy with his bag slung over his shoulder so as you can't get
past, and you nudge it a bit to let him know and he looks at
you like, 'What the fuck are you doing to my bag?' And
you think about saying 'You're the one with it in my
fucking way, arsehole,' but you don't. The doors close and
you miss your stop.

Later, on the escalator, people are standing on the left like
they don't give a fuck and you feel like grabbing 'em by the
collar and toppling 'em right down to the bottom. But you
don't.

And then in Starbucks the guy at the till writing out a
cheque – a fucking *cheque* in this day an age – and there's
a queue of about eighty people and you wanna grab the
fucking thing out of his hands and shove it up his hairy
arse. But you don't.

And at the zebra crossing outside the office the cars don't
stop so you just walk out anyway and the Mondeo screeches
to a halt almost taking your legs with it and the suit inside
looking at you like a piece of shit. And you think about
putting your fist through his window and holding his throat
till the veins pop out, but you don't.

And then the fat cunt on his mobile dawdling along the
pavement in front of you weaving about so as you can't
get past like he doesn't know you're there, when anyone
with half a brain would realise, so he must be doing it
deliberately cos he thinks it's fucking funny or something,
and whilst shoving past him you think about grabbing the
fat folds on the back of his neck and ramming his head into
the post box. But you don't.

And in the newsagents the old dear counting out every
penny like it's her lifeblood and you wanna push her into
the wall of crisps cos you *need* a pack of fags *now* an you
think about running your hand along the chocolate bars and
spraying 'em onto the floor in a big fucking heap, but you
don't.

And then outside in the wind the matches don't work and
one after another after another after another until you wanna
throw the whole fucking box in the air and kick someone,
but you don't cos that'd be a waste of matches, wouldn't it?

And then Alison in the office asking if you had a nice night
and she is so ugly it hurts, and you can smell her breath
even from here, and then your boss comes over an makes
a shit joke which you all have to laugh at and you wanna
crack their heads together like raw eggs, but you don't.

And then at your desk some cunt's spilled coffee after you
left and overnight it's gone into a sticky puddle and you
can't deal with this you just can't deal with it so you go into
the bogs an have a line of charlie off the bog seat only some
cunt's pissed all over it so it goes to mush and you end up
licking it off – piss an all – cos you are that fucking
desperate and you've run out and it's your last dab and as
the piss taste wears off and the buzz starts your mobile goes
an it's Barry an he spent half the night looking for you and

you still owe him from two months ago and if he don't get it, if he don't get it, if he don't get it –

And you hang up on him and switch off and your flesh is is is *crawling* out of your skin an you're just about ready to tear big chunks of it off so as you can just FUCKING BREATHE and you're pulling your fist back and ramming it into the cubicle wall and back and again and back and again until there's a chunk hangin off and there's blood – pale and *grey*, grey fuckin *blood* and skin and you can see the knuckles and it's like they're made of *plastic* and then you slip on a patch of piss and crack your head on the bowl – hard – and you can hear someone screaming in the cubicle next door, and it's right inside your head and this fucking *voice* is whooping and sucking in air an bawling it out again in great howling sobs an WHO THE FUCK is making that FUCKING NOISE?

And you stagger out to get away from it and right into the path of this mad-looking guy and this guy, this fucking guy is screaming in your face an you don't even know how he got in cos the door's locked and he's screaming and screaming and you wanna punch it, just punch his fucking *face* in to make the noise stop this NOISE that's inside your head an under your skin churning into your guts and THIS time THIS time THIS time you do it you do it you fucking DO IT.

The sound of breaking glass.

And his face breaks.

As the mirror breaks.

As your knuckles break.

As the noise stops.

And it was you.

It was you all along.

SOMEONE *knocks on the cubicle door.*

SOMEONE. Charlie?

CHARLIE. Yeah.

SOMEONE. Are you alright in there?

CHARLIE. Yeah. Yeah I'm fine.

SOMEONE. Right. Alright then. You're sure?

CHARLIE. Yeah.

SOMEONE. Eleanor's looking for you. I think you've got a meeting.

CHARLIE. Right. Tell her. Tell her I'll be there in a sec.

SOMEONE. Okay.

SOMEONE goes.

CHARLIE *wraps toilet paper round his bleeding hand and tries to pull himself together.*

He notices a business card attached to the mirror he has just broken. He takes it down and looks at it with horror.

Almost despite himself, he takes out his phone and dials the number.

SOPHIE. Sophie Lewis, Pathology.

CHARLIE. Sophie?

SOPHIE. Yes. Who's that?

CHARLIE. It's. It's Charlie.

SOPHIE. Charlie! I was just examining your knuckles. What happened there?

CHARLIE *looks at his knuckles. A bolt of fear goes through him.*

CHARLIE. F-fuck . . .

He hangs up.

ELLIE, ROBERT *and* DANNY *enter.* CHARLIE *is pale and trembling.*

ELLIE. Robert, you know.

ROBERT. Charlie.

CHARLIE. Sir.

They shake. CHARLIE *winces.*

ROBERT. Happy New Year.

CHARLIE. Yeah.

ROBERT. Good to see you in so early.

CHARLIE. Yeah.

ELLIE. And this is Danny Butler.

CHARLIE. Danny . . . ?

ELLIE. From Sound's accounting team.

DANNY. We haven't met.

CHARLIE. No.

ELLIE. Take a seat, Charlie.

CHARLIE. I'm fine actually.

ROBERT. I suggest you sit down. We have one or two things to go through with you.

CHARLIE. I actually have a a a breakfast appointment with Sound any second.

ELLIE. Yes, we checked your schedule.

ROBERT. Alison's dealing with the Sound account from now on.

CHARLIE. What?

ELLIE. So you have a window.

ROBERT. Charlie, Sound Records are threatening to terminate their contract.

CHARLIE. Oh. Oh right. Um.

ELLIE. He's confused.

ROBERT. It's not confusing at all. Danny.

DANNY. Thank you.

DANNY *opens a file and reads from it.*

On twelfth August our records show you set up a spending account for my client independently of your own in-house accountancy team and without approval from ourselves.

CHARLIE. Did I?

DANNY. There follow some large cash transactions simply entered as miscellaneous expenditure.

CHARLIE. Oh.

DANNY. No receipts were provided.

On first September you invoiced my client for eighty-seven hours over a five-day period.

CHARLIE. Right. Could I uh –

DANNY. Your office security log to which your colleagues have kindly allowed my team access shows you were clocked in at your Edinburgh branch that week servicing an overdue contract with a whisky distillery.

CHARLIE. Was I?

DANNY. However, your colleagues in Edinburgh don't seem to be able to recall your arrival.

On thirteenth, nineteenth and twenty-seventh of that same month some large cash withdrawals were made with your agency's credit card from machines in Farringdon, Shoreditch and Hackney. These were also billed to my client's account.

I could go on.

ROBERT. Charlie, Mr Butler here specialises in embezzlement and fraud detection.

DANNY. Forensic accountancy.

ROBERT. That's right.

ELLIE. Now we know you've been ill recently, Charlie –

DANNY. My client does not like to be taken advantage of, Mr Hunt.

ROBERT. And neither do we.

ELLIE. Charlie. Do you have anything to say?

> CHARLIE *rubs at his hand. Blood seeps out.*
>
> *He looks as if he might cry.*
>
> Charlie, we're going to be requiring you to take some time off.

ROBERT. No need to tart it up, Eleanor, just call Security, please.

ELLIE. Of course.

ROBERT. We're very disappointed, Charlie. Very disappointed.

CHARLIE. They're all lined up. Lookin at me.

ELLIE. Thieving.

ROBERT. Little.

DANNY. Cunt.

> *The blast of a high-speed train.*
>
> SOPHIE *enters.*

SOPHIE. What did you do?

CHARLIE. I ran.

SOPHIE. Where?

CHARLIE. Just out. Out the door, down the stairs, jumpin whole flights like a maniac –

SOPHIE. The bruises on your heels.

CHARLIE. – into the lobby, past Security, over the barrier, into the rain.

SOPHIE. You fell.

CHARLIE. Stumblin over bollards –

SOPHIE. Palm's grazed.

CHARLIE. Clutchin at the kerb –

SOPHIE. Gravel under the skin.

CHARLIE. Kickin at the pavement –

SOPHIE. Scraping of the shin.

CHARLIE. Then up, runnin and away.

SOPHIE. Where?

CHARLIE. Holborn, Cheapside, Cornhill, Leadenhall, shoulderin through suits, round corners, across traffic, stompin into puddles, through leaves and all the time this roar in me ears of London, the freight-train rage of this stinkin screamin town.

SOPHIE. You have a ruptured eardrum. This I can't explain.

CHARLIE. Fenchurch Street.

SOPHIE. You got on a train?

CHARLIE. Standin there in the station, echoey, out of breath, wonderin how I got there, *heavin* the air into me. And all I can think about is me mum. And I feel like I did at chess club after school when my queen got taken. Just that sinkin feelin. Cos you know it's all over.

SOPHIE. A train to where, Charlie?

CHARLIE. Huh? What are you doin here?

SOPHIE. I'm piecing things together.

CHARLIE. Why?

SOPHIE. It's my job.

CHARLIE. There's no point. It's all broken.

SOPHIE. You have a link. A link to someone important. Where did you go?

CHARLIE. I went to the seaside.

SOPHIE. I knew it.

CHARLIE. I went to Southend.

The sound of seagulls, and waves.

SOPHIE. Southend. Of course.

CHARLIE. Mum used to take us. Out through the mud flats
    and pylons, seagulls scatterin at the sound of the train.
    There was space. So much space. And when we got there
    there'd be colours and noise and ice cream and chips and
    live bingo with half-point prizes and grey sand just a bit too
    big to keep a sandcastle upright and old men goin over it
    with metal detectors and 10p telescopes where you mustn't
    look at the sun. And I'd get a pack of Hula Hoops and eat
    them off my fingers one by one.

But it's changed. There's power stations now, and shopping
    centres. Motorways and Travel Inns and flyovers. JCBs and
    plastic sheeting. Chimneys on every horizon. The blue's
    gone, and it's cold. The sea is the colour of the sky is the
    colour of the sea. Green-grey, like bile.

SOPHIE. Who did you go to see, Charlie?

CHARLIE. I don't like it.

SOPHIE. Hey.

CHARLIE. I see it for what it is.

SOPHIE. Stay with me.

CHARLIE. The arsehole of the Thames. Where all the shit of
    London washes up.

SOPHIE. Who did you go to see?

    CHARLIE *hammers on a door.*

CHARLIE. Mike! Mikey? Mike!

    A panel in the door slides open. Eyes peer out.

MIKE. We're shut. Fuck off.

CHARLIE. Mike, it's Charlie.

MIKE. Who? Jesus.

    The panel snaps shut. The door opens a crack.

    Get inside, you pillock.

MIKE *yanks* CHARLIE *inside.* MIKE *looks like he has just got up.*

Heavy drapes block out the daylight. ANGELINA *sits in a darkened corner laying out tarot cards. A crystal ball stands nearby.*

Shoutin out like that. You pillock.

CHARLIE. I'm sorry.

MIKE. You want the whole seafront to hear?

CHARLIE. Mike, you know what you said at the funeral?

MIKE. What you doin here?

CHARLIE. I – I got on a train.

MIKE. Not how – *what.*

CHARLIE. You know what you said at the funeral –

MIKE. I know what I said. I was upset. We were all upset. It was very. Upsetting.

CHARLIE. Well, I'm fucked.

MIKE. You look fucked.

CHARLIE. I am fucked. Things are. Fucked.

MIKE. You're in trouble.

CHARLIE. Yeah.

MIKE. Oh Jesus H. Look me in the eye. Look at me, Charlie. Is it about to come crashin through that door?

CHARLIE. No.

MIKE. You sure?

CHARLIE. It's not like that.

MIKE. Cos if any shit's gonna stick to me you can turn around right now and –

CHARLIE. It's not, I swear.

MIKE. You swear to me?

CHARLIE. I swear.

MIKE. Cos I have got a *stinkin* hangover. And I ain't in the mood for havin to do anyone over.

CHARLIE *notices* ANGELINA.

CHARLIE. Shit. Who's that?

MIKE. That's. That's Angelina. Angelina, Charlie. Vice versa.

CHARLIE. Alright.

ANGELINA. Hallo.

She has an Eastern European accent.

MIKE (*to* ANGELINA). Sweetheart, I'm sorry. Would you mind leavin us for a moment?

ANGELINA *goes*.

MIKE *lowers his voice and paces*.

The mistake I made was to pay my last respects to your dear old mother. It's the little longings of the heart that blow everythin out of the water. And here you are. I shoulda known better.

CHARLIE. I'm sorry. I din't know where else to come.

MIKE. Oh fuck it. S'alright, son. It's alright.

CHARLIE. You got a drink, Mikey?

MIKE. What time we at?

CHARLIE. Half nine.

MIKE. Sure. Why not.

MIKE *gets a bottle of spirits and a couple of glasses*.

CHARLIE. Nice little place.

MIKE. Don't talk shit, it's a dump.

CHARLIE. It's alright.

MIKE. It's supposed to be scuzzy, that's the point. Punters don't buy the routine if everythin's spick and span. They expect musty curtains, sticky carpets, gypsy headscarves. So that's what they get. Looks the part.

CHARLIE. Your – your friend looks the part.

MIKE. She's the real deal, as it goes.

CHARLIE. Yeah?

MIKE. No lie. I mean, I just used to make it up if anyone was stupid enough to walk in for that. Easy twenty quid, innit. But Angie? Whoa. Scares me sometimes. Have to keep an eye on her, she's gettin a reputation. An that's the last thing we want, innit.

CHARLIE. Where's – where's she from? Then.

MIKE. Ask no questions, Charlie. An all that.

CHARLIE. Right.

MIKE. Right. Let's just say she washed up. Cheers.

CHARLIE. Cheers.

MIKE. Old acquaintance.

CHARLIE. Yeah.

MIKE. Happy New Year.

   CHARLIE *downs his drink and pours himself another.*

   MIKE *tries to down his but chokes.*

CHARLIE. Shit.

   MIKE *coughs and rubs his chest.*

   Mike. Mike, mate.

MIKE. I'm alright, I'm alright.

CHARLIE. Is it – ? Should I – ?

MIKE. It's fine, it's fine. Just a bit of fuckin –

   He coughs again. CHARLIE *scrabbles about for something to do.*

CHARLIE. Hey. Hey. Let me, let me – here.

CHARLIE *tops up* MIKE*'s glass and offers it back to him.*

MIKE. Thanks, son.

MIKE *drinks.*

Yer a good kid. I shouldn't really be on the sauce at all, but what the hell. It's good to see ya.

CHARLIE. Yeah?

MIKE. Yeah.

CHARLIE. You too.

MIKE. You're shakin.

CHARLIE. It'll stop in a sec.

CHARLIE *downs his drink and pours himself another.*

Somethin's happened, Mike.

MIKE. I can tell that.

CHARLIE. Somethin's happened and I dunno what to do.

MIKE. You killed a cop?

CHARLIE. No.

MIKE. That's all I wanna hear.

CHARLIE. But –

MIKE. Cos those are the only circumstances where they'll never give up.

CHARLIE. But –

MIKE. Shut up.

CHARLIE. But –

MIKE. I don't wanna hear it.

CHARLIE. I stole some money.

MIKE. How much?

CHARLIE. I dunno.

MIKE. That's a lot.

CHARLIE. But there's also this dealer from Peckham –

MIKE. No!

CHARLIE. What?

MIKE. No more!

CHARLIE. Why not?

MIKE. Because when they come knockin on my door –
whoever they are – I gotta be able to lie convincingly.
Haven't I?

CHARLIE. Right.

MIKE. Right. Plausible deny-ability.

CHARLIE. Right. Thanks.

MIKE. Because whatever you done – and lookin atcha I can
see we are not talkin about a good thing – whatever you
done, sunshine, the fact that you're here means it's gonna
end up affectin me. Because however clever you thought
you was bein. You have left. A trail.

CHARLIE. How?

MIKE. Your fingerprints on my doorknob, your skin cells on
my carpet, the hormones in the saliva on that glass, your
hair on that chair you're gonna sit in. You'll prob'ly have a
piss later and spray your DNA all over my bog seat. You
leave pieces of yourself *everywhere*.

CHARLIE. I'm sorry.

CHARLIE *looks into his drink*.

MIKE. Don't cry on me, I'm not your mother.

I'm sorry. Bad. Choice of words.

CHARLIE. Mike?

MIKE. What?

CHARLIE. D'you ever feel like. Like everythin's sort of fake?
Like you're hoverin over your own head watchin yourself

act out your own life? An it's fake. All of it. I mean, I look real, and sound real, but up close. Inside. I'm like Quorn.

MIKE. Quorn? What the fuck is that?

CHARLIE. Fake meat. Veggies eat it.

MIKE. Right.

CHARLIE. There's just too much *stuff* in the world, Mike. And none of it's real. Like Pot Noodles and Big Macs. It fills me up. Fills me up with nothin. I feel sick. All the time.

My blood's been gettin paler. It's turnin grey, like sludge.

I need. I need to get away for a while.

MIKE. You can't stay here.

CHARLIE. Right.

MIKE. Let's just get that clear.

CHARLIE. Okay.

MIKE. Things are a bit. Fragile.

CHARLIE. Alright.

MIKE. I might be havin to get away myself again soon.

CHARLIE. Is everythin – ?

MIKE. You don't wanna know.

CHARLIE *downs his drink and pours himself another.*

MIKE *has a tentative sip of his and coughs.*

Fuck.

He rubs his chest.

CHARLIE. You alright?

MIKE. It's nothin. Rum gives me heartburn.

MIKE *goes to a chest and unlocks a drawer.*

Now then. You are not in a good place, son. An out of affection for your mother, I will do what I can to help you.

But I can tell you now, you're gonna be needin more than a weekend break.

He takes the drawer out and puts it down in front of CHARLIE. *It is a bit of an effort. It is full of wallets, paper documents and credit cards.*

CHARLIE. What's this?

MIKE. Pick a wallet. Any wallet.

CHARLIE *takes one out.*

CHARLIE. Is this a trick?

MIKE. You could say that. Open it. Go on. Take a look.

CHARLIE *opens the wallet and looks inside.*

CHARLIE. What – notes, coins, credit cards, driver's licence.

MIKE. Take out the driver's licence. Whose face is it?

CHARLIE. Yours.

MIKE. What's the name?

CHARLIE. Daniel Strevens. Who's that?

MIKE. Right. And the credit cards?

CHARLIE. D. Strevens. D.B. Strevens.

MIKE. Dan Strevens is dead. Car crash, 1960.

CHARLIE. Mike . . .

MIKE. It's not Mike. It's not been Mike for years.

MIKE *takes out another wallet and tosses it over.*

Check this one out.

CHARLIE *flicks through it.*

CHARLIE. Alan Northwood. A. Northwood. A.V. Northwood. Your face.

MIKE. Also dead, fell off a cliff as it happens, 1963.

MIKE *tosses him another wallet. And another. And another.*

Mark Addison. Harry Lewis. Steve Middleton. My
graveyard of former lives. My nursery of new beginnings.

CHARLIE. This is. This is.

MIKE. Poetic? I like to think so. Identities become dirty, my
friend. Names acquire baggage. Even new ones eventually
get filthy, tarnished with all the accumulated crap they insist
on holdin against you for evermore. Don't look at me like
that.

The brand runs its course, it sees out its useful life.
Eventually it becomes a liability. A cash cow, draining away
your precious resources. That's language you understand,
isn't it?

CHARLIE. I don't. Understand. Anything.

MIKE. At the funeral –

CHARLIE. At the funeral you said –

MIKE. I said if there's anything I can do. I'd do it. Well. *This*
is what I do.

CHARLIE. Oh. My. God.

MIKE. What did you think I did here? Do I look like some
dago fortune-teller to you? Fuck's sake. It's a front, you
idiot. Angie pays her way with a bit for the tourists, but the
ones askin for me. Well. They want somethin else. They've
been *sent*.

CHARLIE. You mean – you mean –

MIKE. I *make* them *disappear*. But it sure as hell ain't no
magic trick.

CHARLIE. So how. How do you do it?

MIKE. You go to a graveyard near where you grew up. You
look for a kid who's died.

CHARLIE. Oh, no way. That is, that is. Irony of fuckin ironies,
Mike.

MIKE. Charlie, please.

MIKE *gestures at the back room and lowers his voice.*

She don't know everythin.

CHARLIE. Sorry.

MIKE. Just shut up and listen. Someone you went to school with is ideal, cos you'll know a bit about their early life, be able to answer questions.

CHARLIE. Adam. Adam – fuck what was it?

MIKE. Cos that's the clincher – the routine, the *act*. You have gotta live this new life like your own.

CHARLIE. Westbury! Adam Westbury. Drowned in Rush Green reservoir.

MIKE. How old?

CHARLIE. Oh, young. Really young. Primary school.

MIKE. Perfect. He won't have filled in too many forms. So you find the gravestone. Make sure his birth date roughly matches yours. You take down the details, you go to the Records Office. You make some chitchat at the counter about tracin your family tree. Pay your seven-fifty. Fill out the forms. *Voilà.* You have a new birth certificate within the hour. And you haven't broken a single law.

CHARLIE. I'm listenin.

MIKE. It's a foundation document. That an a bit a nous and you can build yourself a whole new life. I'm talkin right up to the Golden Goose, the grandaddy – the British Passport.

CHARLIE. Surely – *surely* –

MIKE. It can be done.

MIKE *takes a handful of passports out of the drawer and hands them to* CHARLIE.

CHARLIE. Fuck. Me.

MIKE. Believe.

CHARLIE. Tell me. Teach me.

CHARLIE *pours himself another drink.*

MIKE. What makes you who you are, Charlie? A name? An address? A random collection of experiences, a few memories? The government starts tracking you from the moment you are *born*. It knows what time of day you popped out, where you popped out, how much you weighed, your mum and dad's names, where *they* were born, the name of your midwife, whether you were premature, late or bang on time.

When you enrolled in school the government started trackin your family's income, your medical history, your IQ, your ability to conform. When you were a teenager and too stupid to know any better you filled in all their forms and took all their tests and willingly handed over all the information they asked for just so as you could drive or go to college or sign on.

Charlie Hunt is nothin more than a collection of pieces of paper. Yellowing, faded, curled up in a filing cabinet. You made him, but he isn't you. Learn how to supply the bureaucrats with a shiny new collection, and they'll leave you in peace for the rest of your days and instead hound someone who's long ago ceased to exist.

You *are* who you can *prove* you are. You *are* what people *think*. An that's the easiest thing in the world to change.

CHARLIE. You should've been a preacher.

MIKE. I have been. Nice little earner. And no, I'm not gonna tell ya.

CHARLIE. Huh. What comes first?

MIKE. First. You max out your credit cards in your current identity.

CHARLIE. That's already taken care of.

MIKE. Good. Clear out the bank too, right up to the hilt. May as well take advantage of kissin yourself goodbye. Then, do the birth-certificate thing. Next, you go about settin up new credit. The key thing here is the mail drop.

He hands CHARLIE *a business card.*

Virtual Office Management. There's a number of places, but this is the one I use. It costs small change, comparatively. You get a secretarial service on a private number, to answer as per your instructions. I get mine to say I'm always in a meeting, sounds busy. You also get about fifty e-mail addresses, but most valuable for our purposes – a central London mailing address.

CHARLIE. They forward stuff on?

MIKE. Anywhere in the world.

CHARLIE. Discreet?

MIKE. As a G-string.

CHARLIE. I'm listenin.

MIKE. So. You have your address. Next, you buy an appliance.

CHARLIE. What, like a –

MIKE. Anythin. Kettle, toaster, whatever. What you're after is the little card inside: 'Fill in this form to guarantee your product.' Bollocks, it's guaranteed already, they just wanna bombard you with crap.

CHARLIE. They're a very useful market research tool, actually.

MIKE. Well, whatever. You fill in your new name and address, and wait for all the crap to start arrivin addressed to Mickey Mouse. Three to six months, you'll be offered a credit card in that name.

CHARLIE. That'll never work.

MIKE *grabs a fistful of credit cards from the drawer and lets them fall.*

MIKE. Uh? You what? Think outside the box, Charlie. Fight the indoctrination. We are turnin the *system* around on *itself*.

CHARLIE. O-kay.

MIKE. But you don't like that way? Alright, credit unions. Borrow your own money, pay it back, bingo – Mickey

Mouse has a credit history. Cheap jewellers are another good one. Go into H. Samuel or whatever crappy store and buy some twenty-pound piece of tat on the instalment plan. Go in each time, pay cash, use them as a reference for your Debenham's store card. Use *that* as a reference for your Mastercard. Use *that* and your birth certificate as ID for a loan.

CHARLIE. It can't be this easy.

MIKE. Believe. They want to fuck you, all you have to do is lie back and spread your legs.

MIKE *takes out more and more documents from the drawer and hands them over, faster and faster and faster.*

It's about building up your portfolio, bit by bit. I've taken my driving test *seven* times – passed every time. Here. I've got mail-order university degrees in Management and Business, Sociology, English, Maths and fuckin some sort of Engineerin, I don't even know what that one is. I ain't never set foot in a university in me life, 'cept to fuck a student.

I've had jobs all over the place – I've been a fisherman, I've dealt cars, I've done property, construction, photography, mail-order porn, whatever it takes to get by. I move with the times. I've almost been done for tax evasion, professional negligence, benefit fraud, under-age models, manslaughter – you name it, it's been slung in my direction. Each time: where's Dan Strevens? Oh, he's disappeared. I've been declared dead on *three separate occasions*.

This way, my friend, if things fuck up *it doesn't matter*.

You start again.

CHARLIE. I like you, Mike.

MIKE. I like you too, Charlie.

CHARLIE. You don't judge.

MIKE. I don't judge anyone, son. People fuck up. Why should I care? It's human.

MIKE *takes an envelope out of the drawer and offers it to* CHARLIE.

CHARLIE. What's this?

MIKE. A little summing. To get ya started.

CHARLIE *looks inside. It is full of cash.*

CHARLIE (*touched*). Mike.

MIKE. The first few weeks are hard. Really hard. You'll need new clothes, hotel charges, deposit for a flat. Food. Crappy cheap food. And booze. Lots of it.

CHARLIE. But this is – [too much]

MIKE. Take it. Believe me. Take it.

Pause. CHARLIE *fingers the cash.*

CHARLIE. I can't.

MIKE. Why not?

CHARLIE. Just. I can't do it. Not now.

MIKE. 'Not now, not now, not now.' Well when, then? When? Because the day after you say 'that's enough' – it's *then* that you suddenly see the rest of your life stretchin away ahead of you. That day, my friend, will be the happiest day of your life. Your new life. Believe.

CHARLIE. And what happens to Charlie Hunt? Did he never exist?

MIKE. Oh, he existed. Records will show he existed. He was not a happy man. He had a tragic and unfulfilling life, floggin a flimsy dream to the masses. One day, he stood in front of the mirror. He held his fingers out. Pushed at the surface. And like cling film, it gave way. He carried on pushin. Stepped right through. Never. To be seen. Again.

Pause. CHARLIE *stares at* MIKE.

Suddenly, MIKE *snaps his hand in front of* CHARLIE's *face and curls it into a fist, like catching a fly.*

I caught your gaze.

MIKE *uncurls his fist and blows a cloud of glitter from his palm.*

CHARLIE. Huh.

MIKE. There's little bits of magic in the world, Charlie. Don't ever forget that.

CHARLIE *catches some glitter and examines it. Some of it falls onto the cash he is holding.*

CHARLIE (*of the cash*). I can't take this.

MIKE. Course you can.

CHARLIE. It's too much.

MIKE. It's not nearly enough. Think of it as an old debt.

CHARLIE. Eh?

MIKE. To your mother.

CHARLIE. Fuck!

MIKE. What?

CHARLIE. Mum!

MIKE. What about her?

CHARLIE. I left her on me desk!

MIKE. What you talkin about, she's dead.

CHARLIE. No, her urn, her ashes!

MIKE. Oh God, Charlie –

CHARLIE. Fuck!

MIKE. At work?

CHARLIE. I've gotta go back.

MIKE. Charlie, listen to me –

CHARLIE. I've got to!

MIKE. No! This is the main thing that fucks it up, Charlie, and listen to me when I say this – you must cut *all* links, and I mean *all*. You don't even go back to your flat tonight, you

get a cheap hotel in a name of your choice and you pay in
cash. I'm talking the works. You even delete yourself from
Friends Reunited. You do this properly, or not at all.

Mistake I made was payin my last to your dear old mother
an runnin into you. Now I ain't sayin I ain't glad to see ya,
but I had a moment of weakness, and here you are. A thing
to deal with. A thing from the past.

You grit your teeth. You stare the loneliness in the face.
Become a Buddhist if that's what it takes. But you gotta
trust. You don't need *stuff*. And you certainly don't need
people. It will make you stronger.

Small pause.

CHARLIE. I miss her.

MIKE. I know, son. We all do. But you gotta take that pain,
and learn to love it. Because it's about to become your best
friend.

CHARLIE *tries to pull himself together but something else
is on his mind.*

CHARLIE. Mike. I've been seein this girl.

MIKE. That. Can fuck things up.

CHARLIE. No, I don't mean like that, I mean I've been *seein*
her – like –

He stops.

MIKE. What?

CHARLIE *(quietly)*. Sometimes I think I'm goin mad.

MIKE. Hey. Hey.

CHARLIE. Losin it, like proper losin it.

CHARLIE *cries. Awkwardly,* MIKE *goes to him and gives
him a manly embrace.*

MIKE. You ain't goin mad, son. You're just in a bad place.

CHARLIE. Mike?

MIKE. Yes, son?

CHARLIE. Can I ask you a question?

MIKE. Be my guest.

CHARLIE. How – how did you know Mum? Exactly?

Pause.

MIKE. We was. Good mates.

CHARLIE. Mike. Are you. Are you my dad?

Pause.

MIKE *indicates the watch on* CHARLIE*'s wrist.*

MIKE. Where did you get that watch?

CHARLIE. What? This?

MIKE. Yeah.

CHARLIE. I found it.

MIKE. You found it.

CHARLIE. On a Tube.

MIKE. On a Tube.

A phone rings offstage, one of the old-fashioned bell types.

I had one just like it.

CHARLIE. There's an engraving.

CHARLIE *takes it off and reads.*

'Harry Lewis. On your twenty-first. Twelfth of the seventh – '

MIKE. 1975.

The phone stops ringing. MIKE *takes the watch from* CHARLIE *and examines it.*

CHARLIE. Yeah.

MIKE. Well, would ya look at that. The pieces of ourselves we leave behind.

Reminds me. Good tip. Get engravings done. People trust an engraving.

He hands the watch back.

Keep it. Harry Lewis is dead.

I've been many things in my time, son. But your dad ain't one of 'em.

ANGELINA *enters.*

ANGELINA. Tony?

MIKE. Yes, love?

ANGELINA. There is a phone call.

MIKE. Thank you. (*To* CHARLIE.) Excuse me, would you? I need to take this.

MIKE *goes.*

ANGELINA *and* CHARLIE/ADAM *look at each other.*

ADAM. Hi.

ANGELINA. Hello.

ADAM. I'm. Adam. I'm Adam.

ANGELINA. Adam.

ADAM. Yeah.

ANGELINA. The first man.

ADAM. I hadn't thought of that.

ANGELINA. Please to meet you. Adam.

The sound of static.

ANGELINA *goes.*

End of Act One.

ACT TWO

The sound of a moving train fades in.

ADAM stands in a train toilet, in front of a mirror. He has a bag of second-hand clothes with him. During the following, he changes into the clothes in the bag. They are a different style from those he was wearing before.

The soft 'beep-boop' sound of someone dialling a phone number. After one ring a recorded voicemail message kicks in.

CHARLIE. Hi, it's me. Sorry I can't get to the phone, probably in a meeting. You know what to do.

A beep.

OLDER MAN'S VOICE 1. Charlie? It's Robert here.

I just wanted to let you know we've got your mum's ashes. Left them on your desk, didn't you? After your shock exit.

Now I'm not gonna pretend we're not pressing charges; I'm not a big fan of having the piss taken out of me. But I just wanted to let you know they're here. She's here. Your old mum. If you ever want to come back. Let's hope the cleaners don't do anything daft with her, eh?

Such a shame. You were one of our best. Once.

A beep.

ELECTRONIC VOICE. Message deleted. Next. New message.

MAN'S VOICE 1. Charlie, it's Barry. Now I don't pretend to enjoy havin to break people's legs, but if that's what it takes then the will is there. So. Twelve grand by the weekend. Understood?

ELECTRONIC VOICE. Message deleted. You have no more messages.

MIKE *enters and holds out his hand.*

MIKE. Discard all your wordly possessions, except cash.

ADAM *takes the envelope of cash out of his wallet and hands the wallet to* MIKE.

ADAM. When it comes, it isn't with a scream.

MIKE. Take the SIM card out of your phone and snap it in half.

ADAM *dismantles his mobile phone while* MIKE *flicks through the wallet.*

ADAM. Or a crash.

MIKE. Throw the rest away.

ADAM. Or a swell of strings.

ADAM *drops the pieces of the phone into the toilet.*

MIKE *finds a bag of cocaine in the wallet, which he dangles for a moment.*

MIKE. Take only what you need

ADAM *snatches it from him and tucks it into the cash envelope.*

ADAM. There's no special effects

MIKE. The barest essentials to get you through

ADAM. No CGI.

MIKE *takes out the credit cards from the wallet.*

MIKE. Don't be tempted to hold on to a credit card for 'emergencies'.

ADAM. There's no fireworks.

MIKE. Use it, and you may as well let off a flare.

ADAM. No clouds of tear gas.

MIKE. Cut them up.

MIKE *hands over a pair of scissors.*

ADAM. No sharpened steel.

MIKE. Cut them all up.

ADAM *does so*.

ADAM. No chokin sobs of rage or pain.

MIKE. Flush 'em.

ADAM. It's quiet.

MIKE. Or burn 'em.

ADAM. And calm.

MIKE. Drop each piece into a different bin.

ADAM. And a bit sad, like all goodbyes.

MIKE. Buy some clothes you wouldn't normally wear.

ADAM. Like with an ex who'd become an ex years ago.

MIKE. Dark, second-hand, unnoticeable.

ADAM. Without either of you actually admittin.

MIKE. Get changed somewhere discreet.

ADAM. Stayin together out of habit, but knowin it wasn't right.

MIKE. Cut your old clothes up into pieces and flush them too.

ADAM *cuts his old clothes into pieces and drops them into the toilet bowl too*.

Abandon your car. Don't push it off a cliff or into a lake, this ain't Hollywood – it'll be found.

ADAM. Someone you knew intimately.

MIKE. Don't borrow a car.

ADAM. But out of habit rather than love.

MIKE. Don't even *think* about nickin one.

ADAM. And so you hate them all the more.

MIKE. You will be caught.

ADAM. Because you understand completely why they're such a fuckin wanker.

MIKE. You are cool.

ADAM. Cos they *are* you.

MIKE. Calm.

ADAM. Your other half.

MIKE. Collected. An ordinary citizen on the way to work.

ADAM. Someone who embarrassed you at parties.

MIKE. Respectable, clean, average.

ADAM. Said the wrong things.

MIKE. Don't *tell* anyone what you are doin.

ADAM. Lived in the wrong area.

MIKE. Don't ask for *shelter.*

ADAM. Got the wrong idea.

MIKE. Don't call to say *goodbye*.

ADAM. Drank too much.

MIKE. Don't stop for a *drink*.

ADAM. Cared too little.

MIKE. You are hardened.

ADAM. Fell over too early and puked in the water feature.

MIKE. You are on your own. Leave town. Now.

ADAM. Someone who showed you up, knocked you down and locked you out. They erode you slowly, like acid, people like that. You want them to fuck off and die, but you can't quite bring yourself to kill them.

MIKE. Every single place you go, you will leave pieces of yourself. Every piece of clothin, every doorknob, every carpet, telephone, toilet seat will contain pieces of you. Alcohol cuts through this. Use it.

ADAM *wets a rag with some spirits from the bottle and wipes down the surface in front of him. He swigs from the bottle of spirits as he does so.*

ADAM. Charlie will always be out there somewhere. Not quite dead, not quite alive. Wanderin the world. Alone.

ADAM *sticks his head into the toilet bowl and flushes it. He restyles his wet hair.*

Now that he's gone, I get rid of his hair.

I get rid of his clothes.

I cover his eyes.

He puts on tinted glasses. By now, he looks very different from before.

By the time I arrive, Charlie Hunt has completely disappeared.

I go to a graveyard to pay my respects.

The sound fades into falling rain. It sounds a bit like static.

ADAM *steps off the train and into a graveyard. He takes the bottle of spirits with him.*

He examines different headstones.

MIKE. One of the first things you'll discover is that there's no correlation between birth and death in this country. No one thinks to match up the certificates, because no one cares if you die. There's a brief nod of the head in acknowledgement of your birth, but by the time you die, they've simply lost interest.

This loophole is large enough for several thousand people a year to walk right into. The disappeared. The missing. The silent comrades you never meet.

ADAM *stops in front of one headstone in particular.*

ADAM. Adam Westbury. Beloved son of Alan and Margaret. Taken away August 23rd 1985, aged eight.

He notes down the details.

We had an assembly.

PRIEST *enters. He stands next to* ADAM *and looks at the headstone.*

PRIEST. Our bodies are a collection of common chemicals. Mostly carbon with a dash of phosphorus. Enough iron to make a six-inch nail and enough sulphur to rid one dog of fleas. All held together with about fifty kilograms of water. When reduced to dust, we fit into a box the size of an ordinary house brick.

ADAM. I didn't know that.

PRIEST. They teach us this. They teach us this as proof that the body is weak. Mortal. Designed to be temporary. That there is a plan in which it is intended for us to move on.

ADAM. I've never believed that. Does that mean I'm goin to hell?

PRIEST. Aren't we there?

Aren't we there already?

Pause.

ADAM *holds the bottle out.*

A moment.

Then PRIEST *takes it and drinks.*

I, I, I used to think life was like the Bible. I saw beginnings, waited for middles and and and *prayed* for endings. I waited for all the shards of pain and tragedy to come back round again in some divinely planned climax of meaning and truth. But they didn't. They don't.

We stumble from day to day believing that the passage of time indicates movement. Don't we? But it's simply another day.

I just walked out on a service.

ADAM. In there?

PRIEST *nods.*

Wow. Are you gonna go back in?

PRIEST. I don't know.

PRIEST *hands the bottle back to* ADAM.

ADAM *swigs from it and passes it back.*

PRIEST *takes it and drinks.*

He looks up.

Have you noticed how yew trees suck the light out of the day?

PRIEST *goes.*

ADAM *watches him go.*

MIKE. Ignore people like that. They cannot help you.

ADAM. He took my drink.

MIKE. Exactly.

Now that you've found your inner dead child, take a deep breath and a run-up. Because it's time to run the gauntlet of bureaucracy. The trick here is to verse yourself in The Ways of the Bureaucrat.

BUREAUCRAT 1 *enters.*

Chapter One. The birth certificate. Your average Records Office clerk will be bored, and hence predictable. He or she will also possess a strong desire to exercise power over you, and to brown-nose the boss, by sellin you somethin you don't need. They can be manipulated easily.

ADAM *goes up to the counter where* BUREAUCRAT 1 *is working.*

I will show you how this works by first of all showin you how it don't work. Here's what to do if you definitely want a hard time. Go into the vital statistics office and say:

ADAM. Hello.

BUREAUCRAT 1. Good morning.

MIKE. Smile confidently.

ADAM *smiles confidently.*

Then cut to the chase.

ADAM. I'd like a copy of Adam Westbury's birth certificate, please.

MIKE. The typical response from the bureaucrat will be:

BUREAUCRAT 1. Why? Who the hell are you? Are you Adam Westbury? Why do you want a copy of his birth certificate?

MIKE. The birth certificate is a public document, but try tellin this to the bureaucrat.

ADAM. I – [think you'll find]

BUREAUCRAT 1. That's it. I'm calling the police.

MIKE. No no no no no. The way to do it is to call upon what you know about the psychological make-up of the bureaucrat. Walk up to her meekly. Act stupid. This way, she will know she is superior. Say:

ADAM. Excuse me, miss.

BUREAUCRAT 1. Yes?

ADAM. Um, I was just doin some research on my family tree and I found a birth record I'd like a photocopy of.

MIKE. The bureaucrat will respond in a superior tone to show you how little you know.

BUREAUCRAT 1. We can't issue photocopies. We only issue certified originals at eleven pounds fifty each.

MIKE. That's gone up.

ADAM. Fuckin 'ell.

MIKE. But don't say that. Look sheepish and say:

ADAM. Gosh, well. I'm new at this.

MIKE. Widen your eyes. Stick your lower lip out.

ADAM. Is there really no other way?

MIKE. She will educate you by tellin you:

BUREAUCRAT 1. Of course there's no other way. We can't just go photocopying certificates with all the fraud that goes on these days.

MIKE. To which you respond:

ADAM. Oh, well I guess if there's no other way, I'll have to pay the fee.

MIKE. And you pay. Cash, naturally.

ADAM *pays*. BUREAUCRAT 1 *rubber-stamps some forms with excessive force*.

You will have your birth certificate in a few minutes.

BUREAUCRAT 1 *goes*. BUREAUCRAT 2 *enters*.

Now. How's your drivin?

ADAM. Bit rusty. Don't bother in London.

MIKE. All the more reason to book a few lessons.

BUREAUCRAT 2. Just two?

ADAM. 'Fraid so.

BUREAUCRAT 2. You won't be test-ready in two.

MIKE. You grew up on a farm. You've had lessons off a mate. Your dad's an instructor but a bit busy right now. Take your pick.

ADAM. I grew up on a –

BUREAUCRAT 2. Fine. It's your money.

MIKE. They're so happy to take your money, they don't much care who you are.

BUREAUCRAT 2 *hands* ADAM *a form*.

BUREAUCRAT 2. Black ink and capital letters please, or the computer can't read it. If you tick 'Yes' to any of the health questions in Section 5 you'll need to fill in Form D1, and tick the appropriate box.

Another form.

The provisional automatically includes Categories A (motorcycles), B (cars), F (agricultural tractors), K (mowing machines) and P (mopeds). Can I interest you in organ donation?

ADAM. Sorry?

MIKE. Don't bother with that.

BUREAUCRAT 2. Would you like to register as an organ donor to help someone else after your death?

MIKE. The fewer forms you fill in, the better.

ADAM. No thanks.

BUREAUCRAT 2. Fine. Photos.

MIKE. Smile.

MIKE *takes* ADAM*'s photo with a Polaroid and hands the photos to* ADAM, *who hands them to* BUREAUCRAT 2.

BUREAUCRAT 2. These need to be signed.

ADAM. What?

BUREAUCRAT 2. To certify the likeness. The countersignatory must not be a relative or partner. The countersignatory must live in the UK. The countersignatory must have known you for a minimum of two years. The countersignatory must be a professional person of standing in the community.

ADAM. Mike?

MIKE. I forgot about this bit.

BUREAUCRAT 2. Suitable people might include a local businessperson, librarian, lawyer, teacher, civil servant, minister of religion –

MIKE. Oh, come here.

MIKE *takes the photos and signs them.*

ADAM. Who's Father Jeffrey?

MIKE. My Catholic nemesis. Don't ask.

BUREAUCRAT 2. Fine. (*To* ADAM.) Now sign within the white box.

ADAM *signs.*

Ensure your signature remains wholly within the white area. The tiniest flick of the tail of the Y will render your entire application invalid.

MIKE. Keep a steady hand. It's the little details that trip you up.

BUREAUCRAT 2. Fine. Now I'm going to ask you to move away. After a few moments I shall bring my clipboard rapidly downwards – thus – and utter the word STOP. Upon this signal I would like you to come to a full and sudden halt.

ADAM. What?

MIKE. Do as he says.

The sound of a car moving away. ADAM *looks confused.*

Steady now.

BUREAUCRAT 2. Stop!

The sound of screeching brakes.

Congratulations, you have passed. Welcome to the highways.

BUREAUCRAT 2 *hands* ADAM *a driving licence.*

Have a nice day.

BUREAUCRAT 2 *goes.*

ADAM. Shit.

MIKE. Believe. Now. Passports. Not as difficult as they seem.

BUREAUCRAT 3 *comes on.*

BUREAUCRAT 3. Cross this box if you have never had a British passport before.

MIKE. Apply at peak times, early summer is best.

BUREAUCRAT 3. You should complete Sections 1, 2, 3 and 9, along with Sections 4, 5 and 7, if applicable.

MIKE. Every idiot goin to Tenerife troops down the Passport Office two weeks before they go.

BUREAUCRAT 3. Birth certificate.

MIKE. Queues go round the block.

BUREAUCRAT 3. Driving licence.

MIKE. Inside, they're so bored, hot and tired –

BUREAUCRAT 3. Photos.

MIKE. – they'll forget your face three seconds later.

BUREAUCRAT 3. Forty-two pounds.

ADAM *hands it over.*

Going anywhere nice?

MIKE. Don't be drawn.

ADAM. Not really.

BUREAUCRAT 3. Next.

ADAM. That's it?

MIKE. That's it. The new you.

ADAM *examines his passport, driving licence and birth certificate.*

ADAM. What about – what about Social Security?

MIKE. Don't ever try and claim off the social. They will shit on you and rub it in.

ADAM. What if I get ill?

MIKE. You get better.

ADAM. But don't doctors and hospitals check your – [medical records]?

MIKE. Go private. No questions asked.

ADAM. Right.

MIKE. You have opted out. You're free.

MIKE *holds out his hand.*

Pleased to meet you. Adam.

ADAM. Yeah.

They shake.

MIKE. You know, they talk about ID cards. I can't wait. Then we'll only have to go through this once. Here.

MIKE *hands* ADAM *a bottle of champagne*.

ADAM. Oh. Oh, cheers, Mike. Thanks a lot.

MIKE. Happy birthday. So to speak.

ADAM. Yeah. Yeah. Huh. What now?

MIKE. Now? Nothing. You're on your own.

You could even get some sleep.

He gestures at a single bed that has appeared.

MIKE *winks and goes*.

A mobile phone rings once then goes straight to voicemail.

WOMAN'S VOICE. Charlie, it's Jane. Look, I know this may come as a bit of a shock but Robert and everyone else is just going spare here and they've asked me to give you a call, okay?

Now I know things didn't exactly end well between us and I hold up my hands cos I know I played my part and blah blah blah – but the fact is there's some heavy shit going down with the police and Missing Persons and God knows what else. They've even got one of those yellow signs up outside your work. I just can't *believe* you'd be so – be so bloody –

Look. Everyone just wants you to be a grown-up about this for just once in your fucking life and – oh God, I can't do this, I'm just too angry with you! You are such a fucking loser!

A beep.

ELECTRONIC VOICE. Message deleted.

LANDLORD *appears*.

LANDLORD. You can see the Gravesend ferry from that window.

ADAM. That's nice.

LANDLORD. It goes to Gravesend.

ADAM. I like a view.

LANDLORD. In there's the bathroom.

ADAM. Right.

LANDLORD. Got all the usual.

ADAM. Great.

LANDLORD. Kitchen there, little stove, I think. Not looked in there for yonks, to be honest. But everything you need really, it's all here. Won't never have to leave if ya don't want.

ADAM. Does it come like this?

LANDLORD. What's wrong with it?

ADAM. No, I mean, is it unfurnished?

LANDLORD. Oh. Yeah. Din't Jean say?

ADAM. No, no, she didn't.

LANDLORD. She should've.

ADAM. Well she didn't.

LANDLORD. There's a bed.

ADAM. Yeah. That's great.

LANDLORD. What more d'you want? Three-piece suite?

ADAM. That'd be nice.

LANDLORD. Buy it yourself.

ADAM. Well, just a chair or –

LANDLORD. Ain't you got no furniture, then?

ADAM. Um, well. No, not really.

LANDLORD. What, ain't you accumulated none?

ADAM. No.

LANDLORD. How old are you?

ADAM. Twenty-nine.

LANDLORD. I had a houseful at twenty-nine. And two ex-wives.

ADAM. Um, there was a fire.

LANDLORD. Oh dear.

ADAM. Yeah.

LANDLORD. You can get all new stuff with the insurance then. Me an Jean did that when we got flooded.

ADAM. Yeah, I um, I wasn't insured. Unfortunately.

LANDLORD. Oh dear. That was stupid, wa'nt it?

ADAM. Yeah. Yeah, it was.

LANDLORD. So you ain't got no money, then.

ADAM. Oh no, I can pay.

LANDLORD. Can ya?

ADAM. Oh yeah.

   ADAM *takes out the envelope of cash* MIKE *gave him.*

LANDLORD. Cos I don't like havin my time wasted.

ADAM. No, me neither, I wouldn't do that.

   He gives it to LANDLORD.

LANDLORD. I hope not.

   LANDLORD *takes the cash out and flicks through it.*

   What line a work you in, then?

ADAM. I'm – I'm in construction.

LANDLORD. Yeah?

ADAM. Yeah.

LANDLORD. Me an all.

ADAM. That's a coincidence.

LANDLORD. Ain't it just?

ADAM. Yeah.

LANDLORD. Yeah.

> *Pause.* LANDLORD *has found a bag of coke in the envelope* ADAM *gave him.*

ADAM. Oh fuck.

> LANDLORD *tips some into his palm and blows, like* MIKE *did with the glitter.*

LANDLORD. I s'pose this is plaster of Paris then, is it?

ADAM. I can explain.

LANDLORD. Can you?

ADAM. No.

LANDLORD. Get out.

ADAM. I'm sorry.

LANDLORD. Now.

ADAM. I can sort myself out.

LANDLORD. Not here you can't. Hop it.

ADAM. Can I –

LANDLORD. You deaf?

ADAM. Can I have my money?

LANDLORD. Sorry. You've lost your deposit, son.

> *A mobile phone rings once, then goes straight to voicemail.*

OLDER MAN'S VOICE 2. Er, yes, hello, this is a message for a Mr Charlie Hunt. This is Detective Inspector Alan Fry calling you at ten a.m. on Monday.

I'm investigating some allegations made by your former employer, Red Consultancy, of which I'm sure you're aware. Now I appreciate that there may be extenuating circumstances in this case, but it is my duty to inform you that if you fail to make contact within twenty-four hours then a warrant for your arrest will be issued by the courts.

•

So, yuh, if you could give me a call as soon as you get this
I'd be very grateful.

A beep.

ELECTRONIC VOICE. Message deleted.

A bright meeting room.

ADAM *is opposite* NURSE. *She holds a clipboard and pen.*
Medical files are nearby.

NURSE. So. You've been clean for . . . how long now?

ADAM. Uh. Three?

NURSE. Three . . . ?

ADAM. Maybe four, I can't remember.

NURSE. Months? Or weeks?

ADAM. Um. Hours.

NURSE. Ah.

ADAM. I'm sorry.

NURSE. Good.

ADAM. Really sorry.

NURSE. So you should be.

ADAM. It could've been minutes.

NURSE. Mr Westbury –

ADAM. Adam.

NURSE. Mr Westbury. We are the leading private treatment
clinic in this region.

ADAM. I know.

NURSE. Look out the window. A Japanese bonsai garden,
fully landscaped. A laser fountain, a peacock sanctuary,
a cinema, a spa, an organic café. We have everything.
Everything you could possibly want.

ADAM. I want it.

NURSE. Do you?

ADAM. Yeah. God, you wouldn't believe how much I want it.

NURSE. Well, here at Lazarus we run a voucher system. You get to use the facilities if your urine toxicology is clean.

ADAM. My what?

NURSE. One test equals an hour in the gym. Two equals a restaurant meal. Three, a ticket to see a film.

ADAM. I like films.

NURSE. But you have to stay clean. You have to really want this.

ADAM. I do. I do want it.

NURSE. Good. We can help you achieve it.

ADAM. What films do *you* like?

NURSE. What?

ADAM. What sort of films?

NURSE. This isn't about me. Why are you looking at me like that?

ADAM. Sorry.

NURSE. Now –

ADAM. I bet you see some right cases, don't you?

NURSE. I'm not at liberty to discuss other clients.

ADAM. Oh.

NURSE. Now, the course of treatment we're going to embark on is as follows. Put simply, learning processes play an important role in the development and continuation of abuse patterns. But those same processes can be employed to unlearn the cycles of behaviour that lead to abuse and dependency.

ADAM. You've got lovely eyes. Soft.

Pause.

NURSE. We're here to break you down, Mr Westbury. Piece by piece. Discarding the problematic behaviours, then building you back up again. We're expensive, but if you think you're worth it, then so do we.

ADAM. What – what time do you get off work?

NURSE. That's inappropriate.

ADAM. I'm sorry, it just slipped out.

NURSE. Mr Westbury, you are an addicted cocaine abuser.

ADAM. I was just – I didn't mean – God, you make me sound like some pervert.

NURSE. This complex has excellent security.

ADAM. I'm not – no, I'm not some kind of *freak* –

NURSE. Do you want to be normal?

ADAM. I'm not *dangerous*.

NURSE. We could be your last chance.

ADAM. Sometimes I just get – I just feel – It's just been ages since I spoke to someone.

NURSE. I see.

ADAM. Properly.

ADAM *is upset. The feedback begins.*

NURSE. We . . . we can arrange counselling. For an extra fee.

ADAM. I haven't got any money.

NURSE. Mr Westbury . . . Adam. Reception and induction should have gone through the charges –

ADAM. I lied to them.

ADAM*'s shoulders shake.* NURSE *isn't sure what to do.*

NURSE. Listen, there's perfectly . . . competent treatment available on the NHS.

ADAM *shakes his head.*

If it would help, I could call your GP.

ADAM. No.

NURSE. But –

ADAM. You don't understand.

Pause.

NURSE. Well. In that case.

ADAM. Could you . . . could you . . .

NURSE. What?

ADAM. Could you touch me? Hold me? Please.

Pause.

NURSE. I can't do that. I'm sorry.

ADAM. I'll get the money. I can get it. I can.

NURSE *presses a buzzer.*

NURSE. Security will show you out.

The buzzer fades into feedback. ADAM*'s nose begins to bleed.*

The feedback becomes a mobile phone ring. It goes to voicemail.

MAN'S VOICE 2. Charlie? It's Eric. How you doing?

You've caused a bit of a palava here, as I expect you can imagine. Wondered if you fancied another pint or five. Little snifter. Dish the dirt, whatever.

Listen, last time we, uh. I know I was a bit. Well. I know things have been. With your mum and. All that. We just wanted you to know. Well. Everyone's thinking of you.

So. Uh. Give us a bell, yeah?

Look they've not *asked* me to ring. Okay? They've not. I'm doing this as a friend. Okay? As your friend. And let's face it, you haven't got many left. So turn your phone on and face the music, you little fucker.

A beep.

ELECTRONIC VOICE. Message deleted.

The sound of radio static.

PAWN MAN *is with* ADAM, *who looks faint. The radio static fades into that of passing traffic. A transistor radio leaks out some tinny music.*

A table is strewn with mobile phones, jewellery, watches, laptops and other electrical goods.

PAWN MAN *hands* ADAM *a cloth.* ADAM *takes it and dabs at his nose.*

PAWN MAN. Now. You buying or selling?

ADAM is unsteady on his feet.

ADAM. Shit.

PAWN MAN. One too many is it?

ADAM. No, I'm not feeling very – [well]

PAWN MAN. Festive season's over, mate. Get a grip.

ADAM. What am I doing here?

PAWN MAN. I expect you wanted to flog something.

ADAM. I – I can't remember.

PAWN MAN. Urgently.

ADAM. I'm a bit –

PAWN MAN. Drug habit?

ADAM. Everything's a bit –

PAWN MAN. Laid off? Loan sharks? Dodgy fuckers on an estate?

ADAM. This isn't right.

PAWN MAN. Nothin to be ashamed of.

ADAM. I've been here before.

PAWN MAN. Haven't we all, son, haven't we all?

ADAM. No, I mean, this stuff.

PAWN MAN. This? All crap, innit? Detritus of sad little lives.

ADAM. Lost property.

PAWN MAN. You could say that. Yeah. Huh. People should be more careful.

ADAM. Could I –

PAWN MAN. When I started it was mostly mobile phones.

ADAM. Yeah?

PAWN MAN. Thousands and thousands.

ADAM. Could I get a glass of water?

PAWN MAN. Now it's these 'MP3s'. Whatever they are.

ADAM. They're a very useful market research tool, actually.

PAWN MAN. You what?

ADAM. Oh. Uh. Nothing.

PAWN MAN. Look, the boss is back in a sec. If you ain't buyin or sellin you'd best fuck off.

ADAM. How much for this?

    ADAM *takes the gold watch off.*

PAWN MAN. Let's have a look.

    ADAM *hands* PAWN MAN *the watch.*

ADAM. This bloody thing's where it all started.

PAWN MAN. You what?

ADAM. How much? How much?

    PAWN MAN *examines it.*

    It's solid gold.

PAWN MAN. Yeah? So's my smile.

    PAWN MAN *does not smile.*

    This, my friend, is a cast-iron fake.

    PAWN MAN *throws it to* ADAM *who catches it.*

ADAM. No.

PAWN MAN. Keep it. Happy New Year.

ADAM. You've got to take it.

PAWN MAN. Go and get some sleep.

ADAM. No!

A mobile phone rings once. During the following voicemail message ADAM *staggers to a toilet and curls up to sleep on the floor.*

OLDER WOMAN'S VOICE. Charles? It's Auntie Esther here. I hope you get this and I hope you call me back, or send an e-mail or a textual message or or or just get a message to us somehow, yes?

Um. I'm not really sure what to say but.

Deep breath.

Your mother was a wonderful woman who loved you very much. If she knew you'd reacted like this – if she knew what you were – that you'd. Well. I think she'd be rather upset, don't you?

Life throws things at us, you see. Lord knows, it's thrown enough at me in me time with your Uncle Peter and. But what you have to understand is that you can't run away. You just can't.

I'm sorry. I hate these answering machines, they make me feel silly. But please just let us know you're alright.

God bless, son, you're in our thoughts.

A beep.

ELECTRONIC VOICE. Message deleted.

A weak sun rises. Birds cheep outside a window.

ADAM *sits up. He looks bleary and rubs his eyes.*

ADAM. You open your eyes, and it's half-light. In the half-light, your head aches. In the half-light, your mouth is dry. You get up, and light a fag.

He lights a fag, goes to the window and looks out.

Outside is a street scene you don't recognise. Winter sun picks out the cracks in the glass. You look for your slippers, but they're not there. It's cold.

He goes over to a sink in the corner.

You scuff over to the sink, and feel for the tap. A car alarm goes off in the street.

The sound of a car alarm. He turns the tap on and pisses into the sink.

In the half-light, you have a piss. If there was a toothbrush, you'd brush your teeth. But there isn't. So you don't.

You look in the mirror.

You look in the mirror.

You look. In the mirror.

And things. Are exactly. The same.

He finishes pissing and looks around.

You have that feelin again. Of hoverin over your own head, watchin yourself in your own private film. Things happen. You play out the possibilities. You could do this, you could do that. But generally, you don't do anythin. People come along. They take little pieces of you away. And then they fuck off. One day there's nothin left. And you are the *shittest* hero. Cos you let it happen. Every day, less and less. Every day the same.

A radio begins to play, softly. The shipping forecast.

ADAM *looks up.*

As it plays, he tenses his whole body and relaxes.

RADIO. Maplin Sands, Medway, Southend-on-Sea, Thames Haven. North, seven to severe gale nine, occasionally storm ten at first. Rain or showers. Moderate, becoming poor.

ADAM. And you're suddenly hot. Too hot, sloshin up your sides like red waves. Your muscles itch. Your bones itch.

Clenchin your teeth, your arms, stomach, legs, kneecaps, curlin your feet. Feelin like your whole body might pop at any moment and that would be it.

God. You want a line of charlie so badly. And you don't know whether to laugh or cry.

He laughs.

He cries.

He swigs from the bottle, which makes him gag.

He goes to the sink and throws up.

Some MEDICAL STUDENTS *come on in white coats.*

SOPHIE *turns to speak to them.*

ADAM *continues to gag into the sink.*

SOPHIE. So. In summary. As consciousness leaves, he instinctively grasps at the silt and vegetation. In his final moments, instinct takes over and he breathes deeply and forcefully.

This terminal breathing reflex will continue for a short time, during which water and debris will be drawn into the stomach and lungs. In addition to this, the forceful inspiration of water may tear many of the small alveoli deep within the lungs, allowing river water to enter directly into the bloodstream while his heart is still beating. Death occurs within two to three minutes.

She notices ADAM.

Alright. Time's up. Same time next week.

The students go. SOPHIE *goes over to* ADAM, *who is finishing being sick. She takes him a glass of water.*

Hey. You're up.

ADAM. Oh God, not you.

SOPHIE. Here.

She hands him the water, then picks up his coat and folds it away.

ADAM. What you doin here?

SOPHIE. I was about to ask you.

ADAM. I was in these public bogs –

SOPHIE. Well, now you're in my lab. Come on, I need your clothes.

She gestures for the rest of his clothes and wearily, he begins to undress. She takes each item and carefully folds it away into sterile bags.

ADAM. What am I doin here?

SOPHIE. This is where you ended up.

ADAM. Oh God. Is this another dream?

SOPHIE. I don't think so. I'm awake.

ADAM. But you're not normal.

SOPHIE. That's not nice.

ADAM. I'm not a nice guy.

SOPHIE. I think you had some sort of breakdown.

ADAM. You're tellin me. I'm stood here chattin to my pathologist.

SOPHIE. I talk to all my clients.

ADAM. I feel sick.

SOPHIE. Haven't you just thrown it all up?

ADAM. Yeah. Now I need to throw up the rest. The emptiness.

SOPHIE. That's not possible.

ADAM. Neither's talkin to you.

SOPHIE. I'm having trouble establishing who you are.

ADAM. You should try bein me.

SOPHIE. Your body shows all the signs of a high-stress professional lifestyle. But then your arms and hands suggest self-harm.

ADAM. I just wanna be left alone.

SOPHIE. The coat you were found in contained a wallet belonging to a drug dealer from Peckham.

Then again, the ID the police dropped off is for someone called Adam, who we've so far been unable to trace.

And then there's my dad's watch.

ADAM. My head feels like it's gonna boil over.

By now ADAM *is just in his underpants. His chest has an enormous Y-shaped fresh cut across it – a post-mortem incision.*

SOPHIE. Let me show you something.

She goes to the set of large drawers in the wall.

ADAM. Oh God.

SOPHIE. Not squeamish, I hope.

ADAM. Yes, actually.

SOPHIE. Over here.

ADAM. Please get out of my head.

SOPHIE. I want you to meet your friends.

ADAM. I've had enough now. What?

SOPHIE *pulls out a drawer. There is a corpse inside, covered by a sheet. She uncovers the face.*

Oh God.

SOPHIE. This one was found on the Circle Line, just sitting there going round and round. Heart failure compounded by alcohol. It was three days before someone thought to give him a shake.

ADAM. Put him away.

SOPHIE. I thought he looked a bit like you.

ADAM. Shut up, he looks like a tramp.

SOPHIE *pushes the drawer back in and pulls out another.*

SOPHIE. This one we have no idea about at all. Found in a
  cheap hotel in King's Cross. Drug overdose. Didn't have a
  thing on him. Not a thing. The name he'd checked in under
  was false, of course.

ADAM. I don't know these people.

SOPHIE. Another passing resemblance, though. Funny that,
  isn't it?

ADAM. Please. I just want some sleep.

  SOPHIE *pushes the drawer back in and pulls out another.*

SOPHIE. This one was taken out of the river on New Year's
  Eve. Saponification has started, that's where the fat starts
  to hydrolysise. So he probably looks more swollen than he
  would have in life. His skin like a sack holding him in.
  Something had held him under for a long time. We're not
  sure what.

ADAM. Why are you doin this?

SOPHIE. With every single one of these I wondered if they
  were my dad.

ADAM. But they're not.

SOPHIE. But I don't know, do I?

ADAM. He might be happily married.

SOPHIE. He might be.

ADAM. He might be livin in the Bahamas.

SOPHIE. He might also be dead at the bottom of the Thames,
  slowly rotting under a girder with no one looking for him.

ADAM. I think your job might be gettin to you.

SOPHIE. It's the endless possibilities that kill you, Charlie.

ADAM. Really? It's the endless possibilities that keep me
  alive.

SOPHIE. But you're dead.

ADAM. Shut up.

SOPHIE. You don't just disappear. No matter how bad things
get. There are *people* it will *affect*. For the people you leave
behind, there is no *ending*.

ADAM. There's a stray cat hangs round my flat. I give it milk.
Apart from that there's no one.

She pushes the drawer in hard. Pause.

SOPHIE. I'm sorry. That was. Unprofessional.

ADAM. I'm sure he won't mind.

SOPHIE. That's not funny.

Pause.

ADAM. What happens if no one claims them?

SOPHIE. We do all we can to find out who they are. If we
can't, then we turn them over to the local authority. They
get a state ceremony – C of E, I think. And then they get a
grave marked 'Unknown Male'.

ADAM. That's –

SOPHIE. Yeah. Isn't it.

I always found it scandalous that people died alone. Unmissed
and unknown. But I see it more and more. People seem to
wither away now, long before they die. They're just gone.
And no one seems to notice.

ADAM. How did it happen? With your dad.

SOPHIE. Nothing dramatic. Dull suburban life in a dull coastal
town. We used to sit on the beach in red sou'westers and
watch the commercial trawlers on the horizon. They put
him out of business in the end. There was the inevitable
marriage trouble, and debt. His trips out to sea got longer
and longer. I used to listen to the shipping forecast and
imagine him out there. Bobbing up and down in the darkness.

One day he went out alone. His boat was found upside
down on a beach fifty miles away. We got silent phone calls
for a while. I was six.

Mum had him declared dead after seven years. You can do that.

ADAM. Sometimes. Sometimes people can't go on.

SOPHIE. Why not?

ADAM. They just can't. There's nothin left. Inside.

SOPHIE. There's plenty inside.

ADAM. I'm not talkin DNA and stomach ulcers.

SOPHIE. Nor am I.

ADAM. It's the other stuff. The important stuff.

SOPHIE. The stuff you can't get away from.

ADAM. No. The opposite. The stuff that leaves you sometimes. Look at me. There's nothin. Cut me, and it's grey. Like river silt. There's no life.

SOPHIE. I did cut you, Charlie.

As she talks, she goes to him and gently pushes him down onto the trolley, taking his bottle and placing it on the floor.

I cut into your chest. Pulled up the skin. I popped through your ribs with the clippers, one by one. Removed the chest plate. I put my hand inside you. Curled it around your heart. And squeezed. You opened your eyes. And you looked like him.

Trust me. You were alive. You just didn't know it.

The sound of static fades in.

She pulls the sheet up gently.

She strokes his hair.

She goes.

The static briefly tunes into the shipping forecast.

RADIO. Maplin Sands, Medway, Southend-on-Sea, Thames Haven . . .

It fades into static, and then rain against the window.

A mobile phone rings once, then goes straight to voicemail.

CHARLIE'S VOICE. Adam? It's Charlie. I expect this is a bit of a shock. Well, not as much of a shock as it was for me, you cunt. What the fuck have you done to me? I made you everything you were, you snivelling little dickhead. And this is the thanks I get? I was the best thing about you. Without me, you're nothing.

Now you get back here right now and sort this out or I swear to God I'll find you and I'll rip your fucking –

ADAM sits up with a start.

ADAM. No!

A beep.

ELECTRONIC VOICE. All messages deleted.

ADAM. Mike!

A beep.

ELECTRONIC VOICE. You have no more messages.

ADAM. Oh Jesus.

ELECTRONIC VOICE. Goodbye.

ADAM. Mike?

A very long beep, like feedback, or a life-support machine when the heart has stopped. It continues for some time until MIKE stops it.

ADAM gets up and goes to a door. He hammers on it.

Mikey! Mike! Mike?

The door swings open. YEVTSYE is there. YEVTSYE has an Eastern European accent and looks identical to ANGELINA.

YEVTSYE. Yes?

ADAM. Sorry, is Mike here?

YEVTSYE. What?

ADAM. I need to see Mike.

YEVTSYE. Who?

ADAM. I'm sorry, I can't remember your name.

YEVTSYE. Yevtsye.

ADAM. What?

YEVTSYE. My name is Yevtsye.

ADAM. No, that wasn't it.

YEVTSYE. Yes. Is Ukranian.

ADAM. Look, I need to see Mike.

YEVTSYE. There is no one here of this name.

ADAM. There is!

YEVTSYE. No.

ADAM. Alright, you might call him something else but he absolutely definitely used to – [live here]

YEVTSYE. I have been here ten year. Just me. No one else.

YEVTSYE shuts the door.

ADAM. No!

The feedback cranks up. ADAM *cries out.*

MIKE *appears.*

He wears a smart suit but looks pale and drawn. His lips are blue.

His manner is different, calmer, relaxed.

He snaps his fingers and the feedback stops.

MIKE. There's an epilogue I forgot to mention.

ADAM. Mike, thank fuck.

MIKE. Just calm down, son.

ADAM. It's all going wrong.

MIKE. Everything'll be fine.

ADAM. I need to go back.

MIKE. Oh no. There's no going back.

ADAM. But I'm trapped.

MIKE. No.

ADAM. I am.

MIKE. You just can't see the way out.

ADAM. Of what?

MIKE. Yerself.

ADAM. But I don't know what that means!

MIKE. I know. It's a fucker, innit.

ADAM. Everyone keeps walking away from me.

MIKE. Maybe you should stop givin a shit what they think.

ADAM. But you said I *am* what they think!

MIKE. I said a lot of things in my time, son. Most of it bollocks.

ADAM. I trusted you.

MIKE. Yeah, a lot of people did. I'm sorry about that. But therein lies the last and final lesson. See, it don't matter in this life if you're right or you're wrong. It don't matter if you're this person or that. So long as you are *sure*. Like an engraving. People trust an engraving.

Ta-da, kid. It was nice to see you again.

ADAM. Where you goin?

An open coffin appears.

SOPHIE *and* PRIEST *enter.* SOPHIE *is in mourning. An organ plays.*

MIKE. I'm pullin the big Houdini. Disappearin. For the last time.

MIKE *goes over to the coffin and climbs in.*

PRIEST *begins a funerary reading from a Bible, slowly and quietly, underneath the following exchange.*

PRIEST. 'Jesus answered and said unto them: Verily I say unto thee, except a man be born again, he cannot see the kingdom of God. And Peter saith unto him: How can a man be born when he is old? Can he enter the second time into his mother's womb, and be born? Jesus answered: Verily I say unto thee, except a man be born of water and of the Spirit, he cannot enter into the kingdom of God. That which is born of the flesh is flesh, and that which is born of the Spirit is spirit. Marvel not that I said unto thee: Ye must be born again. The wind bloweth and thou hearest the sound thereof, but canst not tell whence it cometh, and whither it goeth. So is every one that is born of the Spirit.

And it came to pass, as he sat at meat with them, he took bread, and blessed it, and broke it, and gave to them. And their eyes were opened, and they knew him. And he vanished out of their sight.'

MIKE *sits up in his coffin while he talks to* ADAM.

ADAM. Mike! No, wait.

MIKE. I'm sorry, son. My heart gave out this mornin. It was the stress, you see. I couldn't cope with bein fifty different people. My body couldn't keep up.

ADAM. But Mike! There's so much I didn't ask you – so much I wanted to wanted to –

MIKE. Listen –

ADAM. Like goin abroad an an an startin a business an gettin married –

MIKE. Listen to me, Charlie.

ADAM. Cos there's so many possibilities an I haven't even started! An so far – *so* far this life, this new fuckin life is exactly the same as the old one!

MIKE. Calm down, son.

ADAM. I've still gotta find a job an an an brush my teeth an make small talk with people I don't like.

MIKE. What can I say? It's not all it's cracked up to be.

ADAM. But I'm trapped in this fucking loop! It's horrible!

MIKE. It's as horrible as you make it, my friend.

ADAM. It's boring!

MIKE. Yeah! Welcome to life. Look, if there's one thing you need to learn, Charlie, one last thing I can pass on to ya, it's to enjoy the little things. Cos that's where the magic is. Brand new socks. Sunlight in the winter. Makin a balloon stick to yer jumper. Weein in the shower. When a restaurant leaves the wine off the bill. The smell of a baby's head. The way lemon juice makes your mouth go. Hula Hoops an Cadbury's Creme Eggs.

ADAM. But that's shit!

MIKE. But life isn't about fireworks and explosions, son. It doesn't happen in speedin cars on ocean highways. It ain't a film, and it ain't a Vodafone advert. It happens in parks, and newsagents, and grandparents' houses on Sunday afternoons. It's the little things that matter. Cos there isn't anythin else. That's all there is. Try an enjoy it.

MIKE *lies down in the coffin. It begins to move away towards some curtains.*

ADAM. No! Mike! Wait! You don't understand! I'm gonna die!

MIKE. We're all gonna die. Don't worry about it.

ADAM. No, you don't understand! I'm gonna die in a *minute*!

MIKE. So what? Have a great minute.

ADAM. But I wanna get away – I wanna get away from myself and I can't!

MIKE. Of course you can't, you idiot. You can change the shell but you've still gotta fill it. I can't change who you *actually* are. I was a small-time crook, not some kinda wizard.

MIKE *lies down.*

ADAM. What if there's nothin inside you, Mike? What then? What then?

ADAM cries. SOPHIE goes to him.

SOPHIE. Ssh, ssh, ssh. It's alright. It's alright.

The PRIEST becomes more audible. The coffin disappears behind the curtains.

PRIEST. Let us now admit this unknown male back into the arms of the Lord. And let us all remember that those travellers who wander the earth with nothing, are indeed the closest to Christ.

SOPHIE calms ADAM.

ADAM. What you doin here?

SOPHIE. I found him.

ADAM. What?

SOPHIE. My old dad.

ADAM. Oh. Shit.

SOPHIE. Better late than never. Thank you.

ADAM. 'S alright.

Small pause.

Soph?

SOPHIE. Yeah.

ADAM. Does that mean – ? Does that mean – ?

SOPHIE. What?

ADAM. Are you my sister?

She shrugs wearily.

SOPHIE. I'll be whoever you want me to be, Charlie. What does it matter?

He curls up against her.

ADAM. I'm tired.

SOPHIE. Yeah.

ADAM. Tell me how I died.

The sound of rain and wind. She begins to tell him, like a story to a child.

SOPHIE. After the funeral, you were upset

CHARLIE. I wanted a drink

SOPHIE. You bought a bottle, and went to the end of the pier

CHARLIE. I wanted to see open space

SOPHIE. You got that little train out

CHARLIE. There was a storm

SOPHIE. The rain

CHARLIE. And wind

SOPHIE. Almost hurling it off the tracks

CHARLIE. I wanted to see the horizon

SOPHIE. But all there was was a massive flatness

CHARLIE. Green-grey, like bile

SOPHIE. You went to the little gift shop

CHARLIE. I wanted some Hula Hoops

SOPHIE. So drunk you could barely count your change

CHARLIE. Tried puttin 'em on my fingers but the wind kept whippin 'em away

SOPHIE. You were woozy

CHARLIE. Losin my balance, droppin the packet over the railin and

SOPHIE. Barely conscious

CHARLIE. Staggerin to the edge and

SOPHIE. Watching them tumble down and

CHARLIE. Winkin out in the grey

SOPHIE. The horizon

CHARLIE. Lurchin

SOPHIE. Like a ride at the funfair and

CHARLIE. Graspin onto the railins for

SOPHIE. Support and

CHARLIE. Feelin sick

SOPHIE. Dizzy and

CHARLIE. And the wind

SOPHIE. The rain

CHARLIE. Like frozen pins

SOPHIE. Darts

CHARLIE. Tearin in from the sea

SOPHIE. Flying up the estuary

CHARLIE. And into me.

> MAN *enters*.

> SOPHIE *lets go*.

> CHARLIE *stands shivering in his underpants in the wind and rain*.

> *He is afraid of* MAN.

MAN. Hello, Charlie.

CHARLIE. Barry, mate. Alright.

MAN. You took some findin.

CHARLIE. I've been. I've had. I was. There's been a bit of business to take care of.

MAN. Hasn't there just.

CHARLIE. Please don't kill me.

MAN. Oh, I ain't gonna kill ya. I never kill a man in just his underpants. I have some pride.

CHARLIE. Oh good.

MAN. Look at ya. What d'you think you're doin?

CHARLIE. I've been a bit. Everything's a bit. Things have been a bit difficult.

MAN. I can see that, you're a fuckin state. Have you been wanderin round Southend like that?

CHARLIE. I don't know.

MAN. Have you fucking lost it or what?

CHARLIE. I don't know.

MAN. What would your poor mother say if she could see you now?

CHARLIE. I don't know.

MAN. What *do* you know?

CHARLIE. I don't know.

CHARLIE *cries*.

MAN. Jesus. I actually feel bad askin, Charlie, the state you're in, but you owe me quite a lot of money.

CHARLIE. I can give it ya – I can – when I – if you just –

MAN. Oh, stop it, please, it's pathetic.

CHARLIE. I've lost my wallet.

MAN. Oh right. Oh well, that explains it then.

CHARLIE. No, I mean, you don't understand – I've lost everythin.

MAN. Yes, I can see that.

CHARLIE. I gave it away and I'm and I'm and I'm – *freezing*.

MAN. Fuck's sake. Here. Come here.

CHARLIE. What?

MAN. Come here.

MAN *takes his coat off and offers it to* CHARLIE.

CHARLIE. Really?

MAN. Yeah.

> WOMAN *and* OLDER MAN *have appeared in the shadows.*

> No, it wasn't so much the money, Charlie

OLDER MAN. It was the other debts

WOMAN. And the fact that you ran away

MAN. A man has responsibilities in life, you see

OLDER MAN. You gotta face problems head on

WOMAN. Face the world

MAN. Be brave

OLDER MAN. Be strong

WOMAN. Be a winner

MAN. A big-hitter

OLDER MAN. Running away is not an option

WOMAN. It's not allowed

MAN. It's not what's done

OLDER MAN. The world hates a quitter

WOMAN. We're here to help you

OLDER MAN. Help you learn how to face the world

MAN. Because you clearly have a problem, my friend

WOMAN. And that problem is us

CHARLIE. No, there's other problems too

MAN. We all have our problems

OLDER MAN. We work through them, don't we?

MAN / WOMAN. Yeah

OLDER MAN. That's right

MAN. So we're here to help you work through yours

CHARLIE. Yeah?

MAN / OLDER MAN / WOMAN. Yeah

MAN. Because you know that we know

OLDER MAN. We'll always know

WOMAN. You broke the rules

MAN. Our rules

OLDER MAN. And without us

MAN / WOMAN / OLDER MAN. You're nothing

MAN. So we have a claim over you, Charlie

OLDER MAN. We've come to claim what's ours

CHARLIE. You've already taken everythin

WOMAN. Oh no

MAN. There's more

WOMAN. Much more we could have

OLDER MAN. There are loose ends

WOMAN. Unfinished business

MAN. You owe us money

OLDER MAN. You owe us time

WOMAN. You owe us goodwill

MAN. Good faith

WOMAN. You owe us possibilities

OLDER MAN. We haven't begun to explore

WOMAN. You can't pretend you're not part of us

MAN. Not one of us

OLDER MAN. That you don't have to go through

MAN. The shit and the pain

WOMAN. The anguish

OLDER MAN. And the terror

WOMAN. Because your pain is our pain

MAN. Your terror ours

OLDER MAN. You grit your teeth

WOMAN. You stare us in the face

MAN / OLDER MAN / WOMAN. And you smile

   They smile.

WOMAN. Come with us now

MAN. We'll tell you about it

OLDER MAN. What we'd like you to do

WOMAN. What we need you to do

MAN. What we expect

OLDER MAN. What is expected of you

WOMAN. What's expected of all of us

CHARLIE. No

WOMAN. We can talk about it

MAN. Like grown-ups

WOMAN. Like colleagues

OLDER MAN. Like peers

MAN. Like friends

WOMAN. Like owners

OLDER MAN. You're part of us

WOMAN. We're your past

MAN. Your present

OLDER MAN. And your future

WOMAN. We're all that matters

OLDER MAN. And all there is

MAN. You can't get away

OLDER MAN. We're claiming you

WOMAN. Be happy

OLDER MAN. You're wanted

MAN. You're ours

OLDER MAN. Face the music, son

WOMAN. Face the music

MAN. Or fall

CHARLIE. Face the music or fall

And so you fall

A short fall

Down into the greyness.

They surround him. The splash of a body falling into water.

SOPHIE. The girl in the shop hears the splash

CHARLIE. The grey giving way, like cling film

SOPHIE. The cold like a toxic shock to the heart

MAN. And you can see your old mum

OLDER MAN. At home she is, in your old room

WOMAN. She's made your bed, all tightly tucked and ready

MAN. Smoothin down the pillow

SOPHIE *wheels over the mortuary trolley.*

OLDER MAN. She hasn't heard you come in, but then she turns round

MAN. Looks surprised, but smiles

OLDER MAN. Says

SOPHIE. Hello, love. Glad you could make it. You're right on time.

MAN. You go over

OLDER MAN. Touch her shoulder

WOMAN. Lay down on the bed

OLDER MAN. Smile as she strokes your hair

MAN. Smile

SOPHIE. And close your eyes

They lay CHARLIE *down on the trolley, and pull the sheet over him.*

OLDER MAN. Sleepy

WOMAN. At last, so sleepy

OLDER MAN. Breathin deeply

MAN. Clutchin

OLDER MAN. Graspin at sand

WOMAN. Let it fall through your hand

OLDER MAN. The softness of skin touchin silt

WOMAN. Close your eyes

MAN. Drift away

OLDER MAN. The sandcastle you built

WOMAN. Is the fortress that keeps things at bay

OLDER MAN. With a sigh

MAN. Not a scream

WOMAN. You finally dream

OLDER MAN. Then the tide rushes in

SOPHIE. To wash you upstream.

The sound of the sea.

The shipping forecast begins, faint at first, but slowly getting louder.

ANNOUNCER. Viking, North Utsire, South Utsire. South, six
to gale eight, becoming cyclonic in West Viking later.
Squally showers. Poor, occasionally moderate.

The others go. SOPHIE *stays for a moment. She strokes*
CHARLIE's *hair, then pulls the sheet up over his face. She*
goes.

Forties, Cromarty. Southwesterly six to gale eight, veering
westerly later. Showers, good.

Maplin Sands, Medway, Southend-on-Sea, Thames Haven.
West or southwest six, occasionally seven in Thames.
Showers. Good.

The shipping forecast fades into radio static.

Blackout.

End.